WALLACE

A Portrait of Power

Wallace: A Portrait of Power

Published by
The Birmingham News
Division of Special Projects
2200 4th Ave. N. / P.O. Box 2553
Birmingham, AL 35203
(205) 325-3188

Book design and typography: Lori Leath-Smith
Cover design: Melodie Chancey

Printed in the United States of America

ISBN 1-57571-006-4

GOVERNOR GEORGE WALLACE

AUGUST 25, 1919 - SEPTEMBER 13, 1998

Table of Contents

Flag stands at half staff just off Dexter Avenue with Dexter Avenue King Memorial Baptist Church on the right and Capitol Building, a state landmark from which Wallace governed Alabama for years, in the background.

Epitath

George Corley Wallace, the four-term Alabama governor who was once the nation's foremost champion of Southern segregation and later a wounded advocate of racial reconciliation, died Sunday night.

The 79-year-old Wallace, who was paralyzed from the waist down in a 1972 assassination attempt while making the third of four tries at the presidency, died at Jackson Hospital in Montgomery at 9:45 p.m. Sunday Sept. 13, 1998.

He was admitted in the hospital Thursday with a urinary tract infection that had spread to his blood, but his condition had improved during the weekend.

Jackson Hospital spokeswoman Victoria Jones said Wallace had had a "relatively quiet day with mild discomfort" Sunday, and by 7:30 his family had left for the evening. Wallace was napping at the time.

Shortly afterward, he began to experience respiratory problems and went into respiratory and cardiac arrest about 8:30 p.m., Ms. Jones said. After more than an hour of efforts to resuscitate him, Wallace was pronounced dead, she said.

"The governor fought and fought hard for his life," she said.

At Wallace's bedside were his son, former state Treasurer George Jr., and one of his three daughters, Peggy Wallace Kennedy.

Wallace's passing leaves a state where scores of schools, roads and industrial sites were built or funded during one of his four terms, and where scores of buildings or other structures bear his name. Dozens of officeholders still owe their political lives to Wallace, who gave them their starts in politics by appointing them to boards or vacant county courthouse posts.

In national politics, the anti-big government movement so associated with the Republican Party echoes the states rights stands that Wallace took both as a governor and presidential candidate.

Those same states rights stands, coupled with Wallace's fiery prosegregation pronouncements, still are part of Alabama's image today.

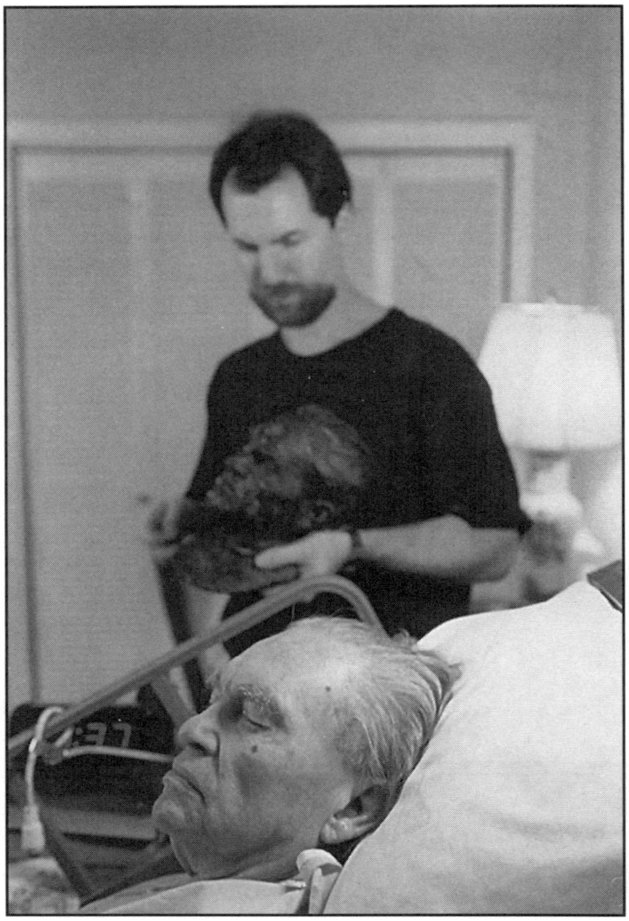

Bedridden in final years, Wallace is visited in 1997 by sculptor Dan Edwards, who is preparing a wax model of the governor's face

Wallace had been hospitalized more than 30 times to be tested or treated for various ailments associated with his paralysis. At the time of his death, the formerly feisty and vigorous candidate—whose presence had once filled stadiums and auditoriums—had not left his Montgomery home since October 1996 except to go to the doctor or the hospital, a spokesman said.

His hospital visits were on the increase during Wallace's final term as governor in the late 1980s.

In early 1986, citing his frail health, Wallace announced he would not seek another term. He took a fund-raising job for Troy State University, was divorced from his third wife, and moved to a specially equipped house in southeast Montgomery.

But recurring bouts of pain, urinary tract infections and other health-related problems kept him away from his office and led to increasingly more frequent stays in the hospital. His eyesight also deteriorated.

Despite his woes, Wallace fiercely hung on to life. Some years back, data compiled by University Hospital's Spinal Cord Injury Center suggested that when someone in their early 50s suffered wounds as Wallace did, they normally lived about 12 more years. Wallace lived more than twice that long, and friends, family members and physicians said that longevity was due in part to good medical care and a desire to keep going.

Friends and family members said that

desire to keep going pulled Wallace through his closest brush with death since he was shot, a septic shock seizure in 1992.

Later, Wallace made public appearances in the newly restored state Capitol, and made campaign appearances for son George Jr.'s unsuccessful bids for Congress and lieutenant governor. He was a regular diner at Martin's family-style restaurant in Montgomery, ketchup and a hamburger steak quite often the dominant fare on his luncheon plate. He also attended a November 1993 meeting of black mayors in Tuskegee.

He also consented to interviews in which, again and again, he said he didn't have long to live and that he never was a hater. He would recount how his time in public office helped black and white alike. He said the fate of his soul—and whether he would be held spiritually accountable for the World War II bombing missions in which he participated—mattered much more to him than his place in history.

"I don't expect people to forget my brash words or deeds," Wallace said in a statement after publication of his authorized biography, George Wallace: American Populist, by journalist Stephan Lesher. "But I ask that they try to remember the actions that I took that were designed to help them."

In his later years, as his physical frailties were overpoweringly evident, old friends

Public appearances such as this with son George Jr. on his last day of governor in 1987 dwindled after he left office.

When visiting the Capitol Wallace often paused at the painting of his wife Lurleen.

found it hard to visit him. His once-powerful voice was shot and his deafness left him unable to hear applause meant for him, unable to really communicate with anyone without great effort. Questions and comments for him had to be written in large block letters that still were a struggle for him to read.

His charisma, his ability to engage a crowd, were gone, his old rooster posture replaced by the hunkered-down, shoulders-up-around-the-ears pose of the aged and infirm. Before he quit going to his office, before bedsores and other infirmities confined him to his bed, he often was forced to trade sitting in his wheel chair for lying on a couch before his work day was done.

"I'm sorry I would be this way when you're here," he said to visitors in recent years.

Still when he managed to visit the Capitol, visitors would be stunned to see him rolling down the hallway or tearfully pausing by the rotunda statue of his first wife. People would touch him, try to tell him of something he had done that they remembered, or have their children pose alongside him for a quick photograph. Wallace would smile broadly at these gestures of recognition.

On his 76th birthday, after some negotiations with Troy State officials, Wallace formally retired from his fund-raising job. But he was not yet out of the national spotlight. It was subsequently revealed that in 1995, he had written his would-be assassin, Arthur Bremer, telling him that he loved him and hoping his attacker would ask God "for forgiveness . . . so you can go to heaven like I am going to heaven."

In October of 1996, Vivian Malone Jones, one of the two black students whom Wallace had tried to stop from enrolling at the University of Alabama in 1963, received an award honoring her courage.

A foundation bearing Wallace's name gave Mrs. Jones the award at a black-tie dinner at the state Capitol. Wallace himself was present, and before the dinner, he met Mrs. Jones for the first time.

In 1997, Wallace Sr. was in the news again because Turner Network Television was filming a lengthy docudrama on his life, featuring Gary Sinise in the lead role. An early draft of the script drew protests from Wallace friends and family members, but when the movie aired, it drew generally favorable reviews. On the night Wallace died, Sinise received an Emmy for his performance.

Wallace, who by that time was bedridden, was initially reluctant to watch the film. But in the weeks that followed, he spent many hours watching a videocassette of the movie, while smoking his trademark Garcia y Vega cigars. Footage from Lurleen's 1968 funeral also was often on his large television screen.

His last public appearance had come at a Bob Dole rally at the Capitol and when he appeared on the Capitol steps, the crowd below him on Dexter Avenue had let out an old-time roar.

On the way to the rally, Wallace's van had pulled off Interstate 85 to take the Union Street exit to the Capitol, only to find it blocked by a state trooper. After a few minutes of conversation with the van driver, who was himself a trooper, the officer allowed the vehicle to pass through. Sitting in the back and puffing away on a cigar, the vehicle's principal passenger told an aide why they had been allowed to proceed.

"Cause I'm George C. Wallace, that's why," he said.

A fighter to the end

A blood clot blocking the flow of blood from George Wallace's heart was the likely cause of his death Sunday, his doctor said Monday.

No one will ever know for sure because the family has declined to have an autopsy performed, said Dr. Alan M. Babb, a Montgomery internal medicine specialist who's been Wallace's doctor since 1992. But, he said, when he and fellow internist Geoff Daugherty evaluated what had happened in the last hour of Wallace's life, they came to the conclusion that all of Wallace's symptoms indicated a blood clot at a lung, a condition called a pulmonary embolism.

]The clot likely broke off from a deep vein in one of Wallace's paralyzed legs, Babb said.

Babb called Wallace "a tough guy."

"He was fighting to the end," Babb said. "Boy, was he fighting."

Closing an era

MONTGOMERY—With somber ceremony, emotional tributes and a bit of humor, former Gov. George Corley Wallace was laid to rest Wednesday, bringing to a close a life that shaped Alabama like no other this century.

"It is the end of an era," said state Rep. Richard Laird, D-Roanoke.

Laird was among hundreds of elected officials and dignitaries who converged on the Capitol Wednesday for a state memorial service for Wallace.

"Governor Wallace was prepared to do battle. . . when he thought it was right. And he had the courage to change," Gov. Fob James told those who gathered in the old House chamber for the memorial service. "That, by definition, is statesmanship."

Former Gov. John Patterson, the only person to beat Wallace in a statewide election, said Wallace's death affected him deeply. "I had a feeling of profound loss, as if a part of my own life had ebbed away," Patterson said.

Patterson said he once asked the four-term governor where he believed his soul would go.

"He said, 'I believe I am going to inherit the kingdom of heaven.' I believe that the governor has done just that," Patterson said.

The noon memorial service came at the

Wallace family members are escourted by military officers, Gov. and Mrs. Fob James

end of a 24-hour vigil during which Wallace's body lay in the Capitol's first-floor rotunda. An estimated 25,000 people signed guest books and passed by Wallace's bronze casket, draped with the Alabama flag.

Shortly after 1 p.m., uniformed state troopers carefully carried the casket down the Capitol steps to a white hearse. The Rev. Franklin Graham, son of evangelist Billy Graham, was among several religious figures who followed the casket down the steps.

Then the hearse, preceded by a military honor guard and a dozen Montgomery police officers on motorcycles, began a slow procession down Dexter Avenue toward First United Methodist Church, where more than 1,000 people gathered for the funeral.

Along the way, small groups of people stood on street corners, watching the procession pass.

At the church, mourners began filing in before noon for the 2 p.m funeral.

An overflow crowd was ushered to a side hall to watch the proceedings on television, but they stood and sang along to the hymns *A Mighty Fortress Is Our God* and *Because He Lives*.

Graham witnessed, praising Wallace for standing solid on his political beliefs. He also sent prayers from his father.

"I believe that if the governor were here he'd want to be remembered for this: 'Jesus Christ today, Jesus Christ tomorrow, Jesus Christ forever,'" Graham said, a new spin on Wallace's oft-quoted promise to preserve segregation.

Wallace's minister, Rev. Lester Spencer of St. James United Methodist Church, said the former governor and King David were alike in their attempts at redemption.

"George Wallace knew when to admit he was wrong, when to repent of his sin and ask forgiveness," Lester said. Alabama and the world should recognize the legacy Wallace provided—not through his stand in the schoolhouse door, but through his four children and eight grandsons," Lester said.

Anecdotes about the family sparked laughter a few times, especially a story about Wallace and first wife Lurleen after she was elected governor in 1966. The pair went to a meeting of the nation's governors in Washington, D.C., Lester said. When Wallace suggested his wife join the other first ladies while he met with the governors,

Lurleen said, "George, I'm the governor. I'm going in with the governors and you can do whatever you want to."

"I think the greatest test of George Wallace's courage was this: That he was willing to admit that he was wrong. ... It takes a big man to say when you're wrong," Lester said. Everyone has a "schoolhouse door stand somewhere inside of us because we're all sinners in the eyes of God. . . But Gov. Wallace admitted his wrong and he asked forgiveness and this took incredible courage."

Troopers carried the casket out at about 3 p.m..

A half hour later, the procession arrived at the Wallace family plot, adjacent to a bell tower at the cemetery's highest point. The honor guard placed the casket over a vault, next to the grave of Lurleen Wallace.

A short distance away, State Trooper Cpl. John Fields played Largo from Dvorak's New World Symphony on bagpipes..

Facing Wallace's four children and their spouses, Graham gestured toward their father's casket and said, "He's not here. He's alive. He's more alive now than he's ever been. He's alive and he's in heaven."

Following a Scriptural reading and recital of the Lord's Prayer, bagpipes and trumpets played "Amazing Grace." Then troopers fired a 21-gun salute as two of Wallace's daughters, Lee Dye and Peggy Kennedy, brought handkerchiefs to their faces. "Taps" was played on trumpet, and the state flag was removed from Wallace's casket and folded. A grim-faced Gov. James handed it to Wallace's oldest daughter, Bobbi Jo Parsons, then gave already folded flags to the rest of the Wallace children.

Four F-16s from the Alabama Air National Guard's 187th Fighter Wing flew overhead. One jet pulled up and out of the formation, symbolizing a departed leader.

The Wallace Epitaph: Power at a Price

I don't know, it doesn't make much difference. Because what happens to my soul is going to be more important than what happens to me in history. I... don't think much about my own history. I do know, though, that I've done a lot of things that I don't get credit for.

—George Wallace in 1991

Wallace draws a crowd in Gadsden during his 1962 bid for governor.

George Corley Wallace spent four terms and parts of three decades in Alabama's highest office—far longer than any other governor.

He made strong bids for the presidency, and planted himself at the white-hot epicenter of some of the most notable and notorious events in late 20th century America.

In the process, Wallace became the defining political figure for a generation of Alabamians and a defining political image of Alabama for the nation and the world.

In the heady younger times of his more than a quarter-century of public life, a vibrant George Wallace seemed able to direct his destiny, and that of millions of followers, with the force of his voice and of his will.

But his last years were far from those years of power. Old, crippled and isolated from the crowds that once chanted his name, he sounded resigned to letting others prepare the final draft of his historical record.

"I don't know, it doesn't make much difference," he said during an interview in his memento-filled Montgomery office on a sunless winter afternoon several years after

After leaving office, Wallace rarely made public appearances, but at the time of this photograph was touring the newly renovated Capitol with his son, State Treasurer George Wallace, Jr. The governor, who said he was still "in a lot of pain," grips his leg as he typically has since being shot in 1972 in an assassination attempt.

his public career had ended.

"Because what happens to my soul is going to be more important than what happens to me in history. I . . . don't think much about my own history. I do know, though, that I've done a lot of things that I don't get credit for." His friends said Wallace worried that his name would be synonymous only with the violence and racial intolerance of his early years in office and not with the good things he believed he had done for all Alabamians.

"It gnaws at him," his longtime friend and Cabinet official Taylor Hardin said a few years before Wallace's death. "I think the greatest concern in his life now—what mystifies him—is why he can't be accepted as a person who has modified his views and changed with the times. He can't understand why he can't be accepted as having done good for his state and his country. If he could have one thing, he'd like to be rehabilitated in the public's mind. Hell, it's going to be on his tomb stone, I think—The 'School-house Door.' I'm sorry he has to lay up in the bed and think about that."

Alabamians, followers and foes alike, surely have that memory of Wallace.

They recall him as the ruler of defiant remnants of the Old South, the defender of segregation, the summoner of the Confederacy's memories of betrayal and loss.

They also recall him as the master politician, an instinctive tactician and commanding stump

In 1963, George Wallace and Nicholas Katzenbach stand in school house door.

Wallace draws a standing-room-only crowd in Winston County in 1962.

speaker who could find the electorate's hot buttons and push them to his advantage.

They will remember the thread of populism that wound through his career. It was a strand persistently present in the way he used state government to create trade schools and free textbooks and incentives to lure industry—all things, he argued, helped the little man, black and white.

And they will remember the national figure, the man who awoke the silent majority before it had a name, and later saw those votes delivered to other presidential candidates who played his themes in smoother arrangements.

Wallace came to power and prominence because he figured a way to harness nearly two centuries of Southern resentment. Long before voter exploitation became the high-paid turf of political consultants, Wallace's own uncanny instincts (and the lesson of a stinging loss to race-baiting opponent John Patterson in the 1958 gubernatorial campaign) told him that the potent steam of resentment Alabamians felt toward intervention and change could power his political ascent.

Using a mix of tried-and-true populism, smug reassurances that Alabama and Alabamians were just fine the way they were, Wallace tapped the pent-up emotions of the

A young George Wallace enjoys enthusiastic support in his 1958 campaign for governor.

Dixie populace. He emerged as the voice of the truck farmer and the coal miner, those sweat-stained and dirt-streaked common white folk who wanted familiar pathways of their lives protected and preserved.

By standing in the schoolhouse door, standing up to bureaucrats who wanted to impose Washington's holier-than-thou will on the state, or sending his state troopers to stand in the way of civil rights marchers, Wallace was standing up for the white majority. His crusade for states' rights held a much deeper meaning for the historically downtrodden South: We could refight the War of Northern Aggression, and this time, we'd win.

It was no coincidence that Wallace chose a Southern epithet straight from the Reconstruction era—"They're scallywaggin' carpetbaggin' liars"—to express his contempt for federal judges. The line, delivered with a sneering curl of the lip and punctuated by a vigorous spit into his handkerchief, never failed to produce whoops of regional pride.

For the nation and the world, Wallace's jut-jawed defiance in the face of the hurricane of social change sweeping through the United States in the 1960s and '70s came to physically symbolize Alabama and the rest of the South. He defined and embodied the region's post-Confederate temperament—its fragile, self-conscious, wounded pride and hardscrabble fight to succeed, its distrust of outsiders and fear of being overrun by change, its romanticism of violence and obsession with perceived historical wrongs.

The truly surprising thing—at least to the political gentry inside the Washington Beltway—was that Wallace's message resonated with voters outside the South. To the horrified astonishment of the Democratic and Republican political establishment, Wallace's early forays into the working-class cities of the Rust Belt drew crowds of hundreds who responded as enthusiastically to his measage as the folks back home in Cullman and Clio.

The gathering momentum of Wallace's successes in Northern presidential primaries as the 1960s raged on destroyed the comfortable notion that bigotry and xenophobia were confined to one geographic region and one people. Wallace sensed like no politician before him that the anxieties he addressed—of outside control, of people who looked and acted differently, of a world spinning into lawlessness and anarchy—weren't just Southern fears.

"Send them a message," he urged his supporters. The message they sent was that a substantial, heretofore silent mass of voters—enough to sway or even decide a presidential race—didn't like the liberal turn the country was taking.

While Democratic leaders shunned Wallace, the Republicans watched, learned and quietly imitated, and the South became a GOP presidential stronghold. The principles of Ronald Reagan are an apt example. The hallmarks of the Great Communicator's campaign and appeal—law and order, states' rights and non-interference by the federal government, and subtle approval of the curtailment of affirmative action—were straight

Wallace campaigns across Alabama from the back of a flatbed truck in 1962.

Wallace shakes hands with the Rev. Joseph Lowery before a meeting with black leaders in the governor's office.

Looking back, Alabama Gov. George C. Wallace says he now feels it is best that segregation is gone from the South.

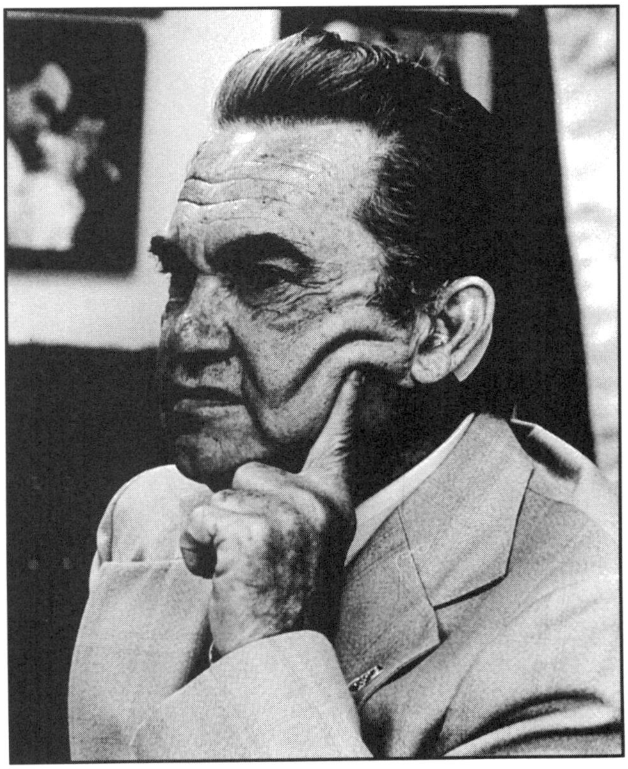

from the Wallace playbook.

In the end in Alabama, however, Wallace turned away from that playbook. Facing defeat in his last race for governor and acknowledging that his attitudes toward racial issues in the past were wrong, Wallace reclaimed the populism of his early political days, professed himself a convert to racial equality, and rallied black voters to his rescue. Wallace's forging of that final coalition of true believers and black converts was worthy of his lifetime of political magic.

Wallace waged a final campaign, one he hoped would persuade history to see more than a racial demagogue on the Capitol steps and in the schoolhouse door.

At his death, most Alabamians have their personal judgments of their state's preeminent politician, judgments colored by voting lifetimes wooed by Wallace's considerable skills.

History will have the luxury of perspective, of course, of judgments less clouded by passions.

> *"I did stand, with the majority of the white people, for separation of the schools. But that was wrong and that will never come back again."*
>
> —August 1982 remarks to members of the Southern Christian Leadership Conference

Barbour County shaped populist ideals

The tiny hamlet of Clio, Ala., is tucked away in the rolling southeastern lowlands of the state, buffered from the outside world by miles of silent fields and stubby scrub-pine forests.

In the mid- to late-1800s, according to local lore, a traveling violin teacher stopped at the then-unnamed trading post and asked about staying to teach youngsters to fiddle for square dances. Hearing that the community lacked a name, he suggested Clio, the Greek muse of history.

At the time, there was nothing remotely historic about the dusty outpost, just a few houses, a general store and a railroad spur. The accuracy of the peddler's unintended prophecy wouldn't become obvious for decades. But Clio's place in history was sealed on Aug. 25, 1919, with the birth there of a child who would grow up to become Alabama's most powerful 20th century politician, a man who would help shape the destiny of his state and nation.

In turn, the setting of his birth and youth—the rural environs of Barbour County—would help frame his attitudes about racial and social matters, and would nurture his political ambitions.

George Corley Wallace was born in the bedroom of a woodframe house without electricity or toilets. It had been built by his grandfather, Dr. George Oscar Wallace, when he came to Clio in 1891 fresh from medical school as the town's first physician.

The doctor's son and young George's

George Wallace, the young boy in rural south Alabama.

father was George Corley Wallace Sr., a small man of frail health. George Sr. had gone off to college but dropped out after two years, returning to Clio to marry Mozelle Smith, a local piano teacher, and to farm land that he struggled to pay off until the day he died.

Young "George C.," as Clio residents came to call him (the local accent stretched and softened "George" into the two-syllable "Jaw-age"), was the oldest of the four Wallace children, the others being twins Gerald and Jack and their sister, Marianne.

He remembered leading a spare but carefree Huck Finn sort of childhood. He plowed his father's fields behind a team of oxen, shelled pecans and picked blackberries. He swam in the icy waters of nearby Blue Springs in a pair of cut-off overalls. He learned to pluck a passable guitar under the tutelege of Cass Welch, a black fiddler, and the pair provided music for occasional Clio square dances. As a small but wiry 120-pound high schooler, he quarterbacked the Barbour County High School football team.

Early politics

Young George's first exposure to politics came from his father and grandfather. At the urging of a group of residents who disliked the Barbour County probate judge, a reluctant Dr. Wallace ran for that post and won in 1928, when his grandson was 9. He gave up his medical practice temporarily with the understanding that he would not seek re-election or other public office, and served for six years.

Also at about that time, young George's father, a hard-core Democrat who would be elected to a term on the Barbour County Board of Revenue, was supporting the presidential candidacy of New York Gov. Alfred E. Smith, the Democratic nominee who lost to Republican Herbert Hoover. The race was a frequent conversation topic in the Wallace home.

Those early experiences left their mark; Wallace recalled telling a teacher in grammar school that he wanted someday to be Alabama's governor.

Wallace got his campaign trail baptism at 13, when he trudged from house to house in Clio to seek support for his father's favored candidate for Alabama secretary of state, Fred Gibson. Gibson lost the race, but carried Clio.

Three years later, 16-year-old Wallace waged his own first campaign, hoping to become a page in the Alabama Legislature. His father dropped him off on the steps of the State Capitol, where he spent the next week shaking hands with as many legislators as he could meet. The lawmakers voted him in.

While honing his political wits, young George also was cultivating a talent with his fists that years later would provide a campaign nickname and bolster his political reputation as a scrappy street fighter. Wallace Sr. bought boxing gloves for his three boys, who set up a makeshift boxing ring in their living room and staged bouts with neighborhood kids.

"I was probably too aggressive for my

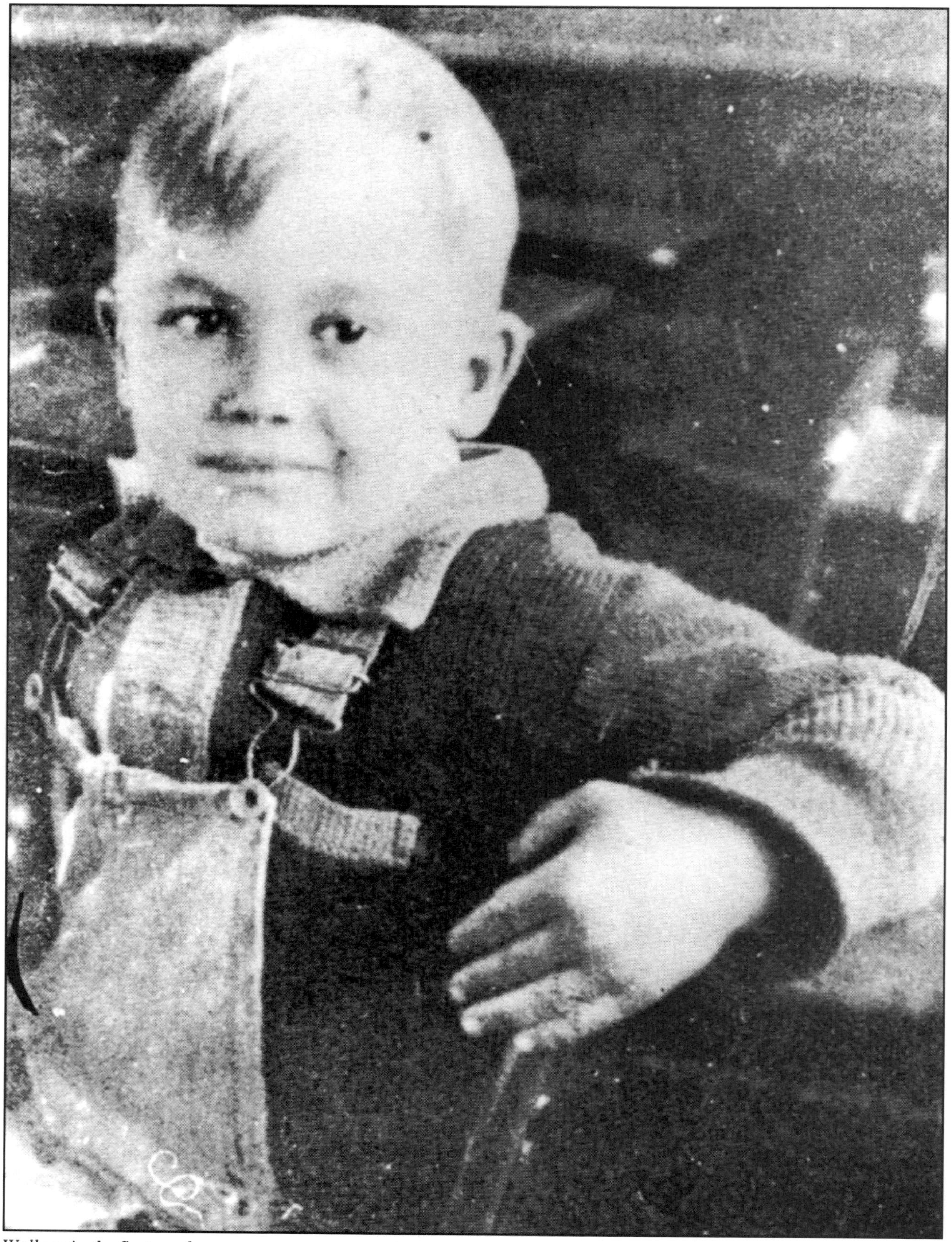

Wallace in the first grade.

Wallace at 14.

own good," Wallace wrote in his memoirs. "But I thrived on the raw, face-to-face competition boxing demands." The comment could easily apply to his future political style as well: quick to the punch, living for the exhilaration of the campaign and waiting impatiently between rounds for the bell.

In addition to boxing, Wallace early on discovered another talent that would aid his political ascension: salesmanship. As a high school student in 1936 and '37, he joined a crew of young men who during their summer breaks barnstormed in an old Model T along the East Coast and into the Midwest selling magazine subscriptions door to door.

In Depression-era America, a magazine was a luxury many families couldn't afford, but Wallace's earnest, drawling patter, dogged persistence and enterprise helped him become the top salesman among the half dozen or so crews. It also earned him $200-300 a summer for college.

Wallace's boxing skills had won him back-to-back Alabama Golden Gloves championships in high school, and earned him a spot on the University of Alabama boxing team as a freshman in 1937. He brought a few items of clothing in a cardboard suitcase and settled into an $8-per-month room at a boardinghouse nicknamed the Bastille.

The boardinghouse was owned by fellow student Ralph Adams, a friend from the magazine-selling crew and later the Wallace-appointed president of Troy State University. Wallace could knock a dollar off his rent for each boarder he recruited, and often used his selling skills to bring in enough housemates to avoid rent.

Wallace spent much of his out-of-class time with pals Glenn Curlee and Frank Johnson, the future federal judge who would become one of Wallace's staunchest adversaries in civil rights cases. But in college they often went to dances together.

Political in college

Fellow students remember Wallace as fun-loving and friendly, but also already having political aims.

"He was a real small, wiry, extremely active, ambitious type of person trying to move into the scene, not in a pushy sort

George Wallace — Senate Page

George Wallace boxing at age 15

of way, but he didn't want to be ignored," said classmate Taylor Hardin, whom Wallace would appoint state finance director and mental health commissioner during his two gubernatorial terms in the 1970s. "Even then, he certainly was extremely interested in a political life of service and had high ambitions."

On Saturdays, Wallace and Adams sometimes spent afternoons in downtown Tuscaloosa, listening to fire-and-brimstone sermons of itinerant preachers to pick up public speaking tips. With the support of his roommates at the Bastille, Wallace successfully ran for freshman class president, but lost to a fraternity-backed candidate for presidency of the Cotillion Club, a prestigious campus entertainment organization.

Wallace stayed at UA to get his law degree, and worked for an attorney while in his final year of school. During one trial, Wallace showed early signs of two traits that would mark his career as a politician: the flair for theatrics and an end-justifies-the-

George Wallace with his first wife Lurleen and their first child, Bobbi Jo, when Wallace was in the army stationed at Alamogordo, N.M., during World War II.

means attitude.

Wallace's legal tutor was defending a man accused of killing his wife by blowing up their house with dynamite. The prosecution's case was strong, and the defense team's only hope was to help their client avoid the electric chair. Wallace hit on the idea of using the defendant's 12-year-old son to gain the jury's sympathy. He sat the boy at the defense table during testimony, and periodically whispered to him that if the jury found his daddy guilty, he would be electrocuted. The terrified boy would burst into tears and hug his father tightly.

Lurleen Wallace poses for a high school photograph.

"I hope I didn't cause that boy any trauma in later life," Wallace said years later, "but I felt saving his father's life justified the crude approach."

He graduated from law school in 1942, shortly after America was pitched headlong into World War II. Wallace, 23, enlisted in the Army Air Corps, hoping to become a pilot. He thought he would be ordered to report for training, but months passed and no such orders arrived.

The wait was maddening to Wallace; he felt everyone who saw him on the streets of Tuscaloosa wondered why an able-bodied young man wasn't fighting for his country. With no income and no idea when he would be called up, Wallace scraped along by managing Adams' boarding house (his college friend was already in the Army). Eventually he bluffed his way into a state job as a driver on highway construction projects, even though he had no idea how to operate a truck and had to bribe a prison trusty to teach him.

One day, he stepped into a Kress five-and-dime store to buy a bottle of hair oil and spied 16-year-old Lurleen Burns behind the counter. A whirlwind courtship ensued. Shortly after he met Lurleen, Wallace shipped out to Arkansas for Army Air Corps training.

A bout with spinal meningitis ruined his chance to be a pilot, and he and Lurleen were married May 21, 1943, in Tuscaloosa while he was on a recuperation furlough.

"I had a happy life until my wife died," Wallace said years later. "We were married (almost) 25 years and she was one of the prettiest little teenagers you ever saw."

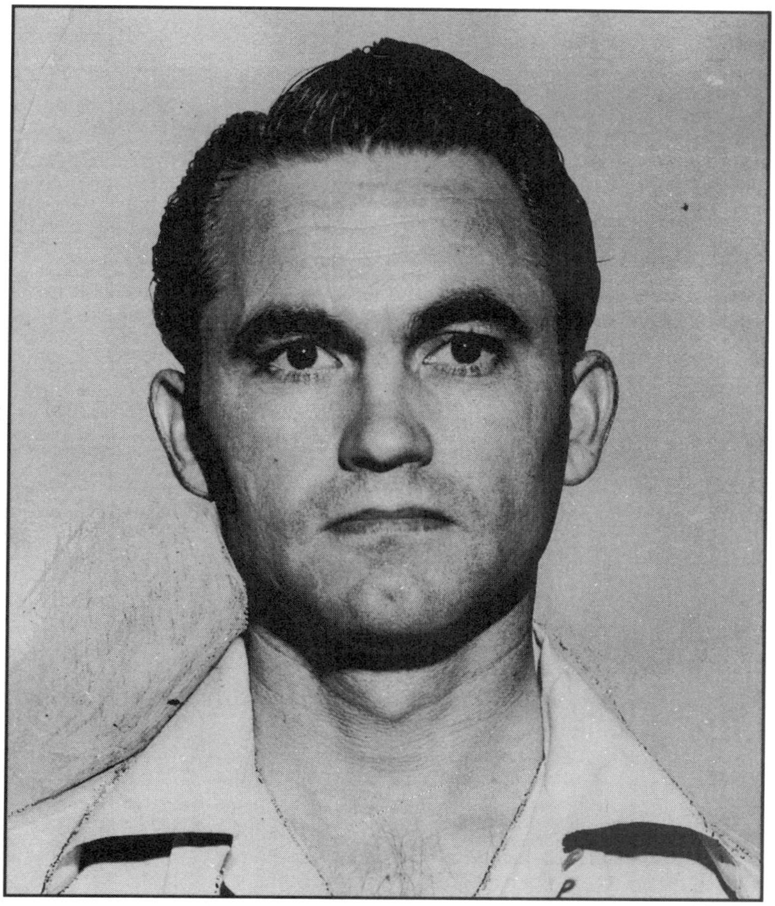

Goerge C. Wallace, Circuit Judge, Barbour County.

They honeymooned with Wallace's kinfolk in Montgomery and Clio, where, to Lurleen's chagrin, he spent much of the time talking politics with the locals.

Even during his military hitch, his future political career dominated Wallace's thoughts. He ruled out trying to become an officer because it might cost him votes later on. "I sensed that if I got back to Alabama and into politics, there would be far more GIs among the electorate than officers," he said years afterward. He took advantage of soldiers' free mailing privileges by sending Christmas cards to practically every Barbour County resident.

As a flight engineer on the high-altitude B-29 bomber *Sentimental Journey* Wallace went on eight to 10 bombing runs over mainland Japan and survived sometimes vicious anti-aircraft fire.

When the war ended in 1945, Wallace was ordered to continue flight training. Weary, tense, underweight and still suffering from the after-effects of meningitis, he refused, telling his superiors the flights no longer served a purpose and he didn't want to risk his life needlessly.

"I had developed what today would be called a 'thing' about flying," Wallace recalled later. "Call it fear, call it anxiety." He was ordered to stay in the base hospital for a special diet and vitamin shots, and was later

George Wallace, Barbour County circuit judge.

Judge George Wallace and wife Lurleen wave to Clayton supporters from the back of a Dodge convertible.

discharged with a 10 percent stress-related disability.

Wallace returned to Alabama, hitchhiking to Montgomery in his sergeant's uniform several weeks after his December 1945 discharge to seek a job from Gov. Chauncey Sparks, a fellow Barbour Countian for whom he'd campaigned while a law student. With Sparks' help he was hired as an assistant attorney general. Lurleen and the couple's 1-year-old daughter, Bobbi Jo, moved with him to Montgomery.

First political race

After about a year and a half, Wallace decided he had waited long enough, and he would run for a legislative seat from Barbour County.

Wallace's political spadework—the handshaking and jaw-boning and postcard-mailing he had done in recent years—paid off in the 1946 campaign. When he hit the campaign trail, his name was familiar to many Barbour countians.

Wallace won the House of Representatives seat, and aligned himself with the populist administration of James E. "Big Jim" Folsom. He served about six years in the Legislature, long enough to make a name for himself and lay some of the groundwork for his gubernatorial campaigns. He also was part of the Alabama delegation to the 1948 Democratic National Convention, but did not join the Alabamians and other Southerners who bolted the convention after it approved a strong civil rights plank.

The Wallace-sponsored bills that became law during his legislative years included part of what today is known as the Wallace-Cater Act. The law enables municipalities to pay for industrial-development projects through revenue bonds and allows tax exemptions for industrial prospects.

Wallace also successfully sponsored legislation to provide "educational benefits" to disabled veterans or their survivors, as well as the bill that began the state's network of trade or vocational schools.

Midway through his second term, Wallace ran for a circuit judgeship that had jurisdiction in Barbour and Bullock counties. Though he won, he kept his hand in state politics by helping direct Folsom's successful campaign for a second gubernatorial term in 1954, and by being a delegate to the 1956 Democratic National Convention, where he helped water down a civil rights plank.

All the while, his aim was to succeed Folsom in the governor's chair in 1958. His 1958 bid would fail, but the experience taught him that the issue of race could be his ticket to victory in 1962.

For Better or Worse, Wallace Always Linked to Race

In December 1969, George Wallace was sitting amid the memorabilia in his Montgomery office, discussing school busing and other topics.

He talked about being able to go home to Barbour County and visit blacks who were glad to see him.

But he also talked about the "proclivities" of blacks: "You can give a black man a Ph.D.," he said at one point. "But give him a few drinks on a Saturday night and he'll want to tear the whole place apart."

Thirteen years later, a wheelchair-bound Wallace, making his final bid for the governor's chair, told a Birmingham meeting of the Southern Christian Leadership Conference, "I did stand, with a majority of the white people, for the separation of the schools. But that was wrong and that will never come back again."

During his heyday, Wallace rode to power and national notoriety on the back of the race issue.

But in his last two gubernatorial campaigns and final presidential bid in 1976, the race issue had been pushed to the background. The tables had turned; blacks now wielded substantial voting clout. Particularly in his final bid for governor, the aging pol faced an irony of amazing proportion: the very people whose subjugation served as a vehicle for Wallace to climb to power could now determine his political future with the pull of a voting lever. Wallace needed black votes to keep his career alive.

Gov. Wallace smiles during a 1972 Miami luncheon when some picketers carrying anti-Wallace signs were hustled out of the dining room. Wallace was seeking votes in the Florida presidential primary.

For years, friends, foes, historians and others have argued about Wallace and race.

Did he believe that blacks were inferior? Did his pro-segregation and anti-civil rights stands stem from firmly held beliefs, or were they merely politically savvy positions to take?

Was his later moderation on race and segregation issues a true philosophical conversion or a change just to ensure his political survival?

And what is one to make of Wallace's support for programs—even during some of his most defiant times —that benefited whites and blacks alike, and would, in their own way, put strains on the state's segregated way of life?

The Wallace era, even in the early years, produced laws that would bring about racial change. Former Alabama Democratic Party Chairman John Baker—anything but a Wallace apologist—said: "Probably nobody has ever done more for schools (or) basic fundamental education for lower-income, lower-class people in Alabama than George Wallace has done."

And Frank Potts, a longtime Wallace friend who served on the state Alcoholic Beverage Control Board during many of the Wallace years, said Wallace had white and black children in mind when he pushed for free textbooks in public schools.

Mrs. Chris McNair, wife of the chairman of Jefferson County's legislative delegation, stops for a word with Gov. and Mrs. Wallace at House dinner dance.

Wallace's inauguration in 1962

Gov. Wallace makes good on his promise to 'stand in schoolhouse door,' ceremoniously blocking Deputy Attorney Gen. Nicholas Katzenbach from entering Foster Auditorium at the University of Alabama.

As Potts recalled, someone opposed to the idea once said, "Well Governor, that's going to cost the people a lot of money. These kids will just tear 'em up and all. The parents can buy the books."

"Well they might can," Wallace replied. "But if you see the little black children in the Black Belt who can't get books, you might look at it differently."

In a 1992 interview, Wallace said that during his heydey in the 1960s and early '70s, his racial views were the same as most whites, not only in Alabama, but in the other states that had supported his presidential candidacy.

The beliefs, he said, were those of a

segregationist, not a racist.

A segregationist believes separation "is in the best interests of both races," he said. "A racist is a Ku Kluxer. Somebody like that's a hater. I ain't never hated anybody in my life.

"I don't hate blacks . . .," he added. "The day I said, 'segregation forever,' I never said a thing that would upset a black person unless it was segregation. I never made fun of 'em about inequality and all that kind of stuff. But my vehemence was against the federal government folks. I didn't make people get mad against black people. I made 'em get mad against the courts."

The "segregation forever" passage, brought to life in his 1963 inaugural speech, put Wallace on the national stage, a stage to which he would return with his stand in the schoolhouse door and his rhetoric of resistance to civil rights legislation. If he was only parroting the words for political reasons, it was easy for him to do, largely because of the guideposts to race relations that he knew in his native Barbour County.

That was the view of the late federal appeals Judge Robert Vance, a former state Democratic Party chairman who often opposed Wallace on issues in the late 1960s and early '70s.

Barbour County, Vance once said, "is about as insulated an environment as you can imagine . . . When you spend all day every day in a city like Clayton or Eufaula, and each white person you know has the same fundamental guideposts in dealing with members of another race, you just don't think about these things the way that people in other sections do . . . George Wallace's world was just very narrow."

By the late 1940s, those guideposts were being challenged.

The nation's armed forces, for example, had been integrated, and the national Democratic Party had put a strong civil rights plank in its 1948 platform.

In 1954, when Wallace was a circuit judge and South Alabama coordinator for populist Jim Folsom's second gubernatorial campaign, the U.S. Supreme Court ruled segregated public schools were unconstitutional.

The post-World War II rise of the Soviet Union and the stalemated Korean conflict added to the upsetting brew. The communist threat was palpable to many Americans, and many white Southerners who wondered about communist involvement in some of the unsettling developments at home.

The ensuing years saw blacks boycotting segregated seating on Montgomery buses; the brief sojourn of a black student, Autherine Lucy, at the University of Alabama; and the federally enforced integration of Central High School in Little Rock, Ark.

And as the racial virus gradually infected every aspect of Alabama politics, seemingly anyone who ran for any political office had to have impeccable segregationist credentials. Vows to defend segregated schools seemed to get the loudest applause.

"If you hadn't faced the race question, you would have lost," Wallace said later.

Just how deeply Wallace held his

Wallace & Patterson during 1963 inauguration

convictions is a question only he could answer. Perhaps, as the late Associated Press political reporter Rex Thomas suggested, Wallace simply repeated the beliefs of others often enough to finally convince himself that he believed them, too.

"I think he learned that racial politics . . . could overcome the shortcomings any candidate might have," said 1990 Democratic gubernatorial nominee Paul Hubbert, who as head of the Alabama Education Association often clashed with Wallace about education funding.

In the 1958 gubernatorial campaign, with its noisy caravans and courthouse square rallies in small towns, whoever won the Democratic nomination was virtually assured of being governor. The runoff for the nomination pitted Wallace against a young attorney general, John Patterson.

As attorney general, Patterson had fought integration, and been relatively successful, effectively driving the National Association for the Advancement of Colored People from the state. His campaign also used a 30-minute film showing integration-related disturbances at Little Rock's Central High and Birmingham's Phillips High. He had the backing of the Ku Klux Klan.

Wallace, though touting his segregationist credentials, straddled the fence on civil rights. He had served on the board of trustees of what was then Tuskegee Institute, the black college founded by Booker T. Washington.

As a state legislator, he had voted against a proposal by one of the state's leading segregationists, state Rep. Sam Engelhardt, to put "white supremacy" atop the Democratic primary ballots.

> *We have our own system of health and school facilities and we'll not have their functions decided by a bunch of punk politicians in a state like New York.*
> —During 1958 gubernatorial campaign.

In 1958, Wallace said that if race-baiting was what it took to get elected in Alabama, he wouldn't seek public office. He denounced Klan support of Patterson.

But if Wallace didn't out-and-out race bait, he left room for voters to think he did. "Keep Alabama Southern" was his campaign theme, and he routinely got his loudest applause when he vowed to close any public school slated for integration.

In the runoff, he blamed Patterson for doing little to stop Autherine Lucy's shortlived admission to UA in 1956, and for not fighting to keep Montgomery buses segregated.

"I was fighting and speaking against civil rights proposals 10 years ago, before a lot of people knew what civil rights were," he said.

Wallace's arguments were not enough to win him the nomination. Things would be different next time, he vowed after the election.

"I promise you, Seymore, I'm not going to be out-niggered this time," former Wallace aide Seymore Trammell Sr. recalled Wallace saying as he plotted his political strategy for the 1962 gubernatorial cam-

Wallace campaigning in Montgomery in 1958

paign that Trammell directed.

Wallace has denied making such a statement, but after the election in late 1958, he seemed to be upholding its sentiment. As a circuit judge for Barbour and Bullock counties, he refused to give up voting records to the U.S. Civil Rights Commission, which was investigating voting abuses. Wallace sensed a public relations bonanza, a chance to openly defy the federal government.

Frank Johnson, his old college chum and now a U.S. district judge, gave Wallace a deadline to produce the records or face contempt charges and a lengthy jail term. Though defiant in public, Wallace sneaked up to Johnson's house late one night with a coat pulled over his head and pleaded for leniency—a short jail stay, which would boost his political appeal as a martyr for segregation. Johnson wouldn't deal.

Before the deadline expired, Wallace quietly made the records available to authorities, but publicly insisted he had stood up to the government.

Defiance became Wallace's battle cry when he began the 1962 gubernatorial campaign. He not only was the front-runner, he was easily the strongest segregationist. This time, the Klan sided with him.

> *We have colored snow, but we separate it.*
>
> —Joking about segregation in Alabama, in an appearance in the early 1960s.

The civil rights movement had not stood still while Wallace waited four years for his second gubernatorial bid. Blacks protested back-of-the-bus seats and "whites only" lunch counters, peppered courts with school desegregation suits, and pushed for federal civil rights legislation. But the Deep South was still resisting.

Wallace pledged to defy any school desegregation order, but said the state would not have any violence. "I am staunch (on segregation) because it is right for both the black and white races," he said.

He also was a staunch public foe of Johnson, branding him a "pool mixer" and a "judicial tyrant."

When the Democratic primary votes were counted, the runoff pairing was Wallace and an urbane-looking state senator from Tuscaloosa named Ryan deGraffenried, who scoffed at Wallace's platform of defiance.

"The quickest way to bring down our way of life is to do exactly what he's doing," deGraffenried said.

Wallace said Georgia had had "a little" integration and the results were "riots in Augusta and sit-ins and kneel-ins." He preferred Mississippi, which opposed any integration and had "peace and harmony."

Wallace breezed past deGraffenried to the governor's chair, but in the fall of that year, Mississippi's "peace and harmony" were shattered by a 15-hour riot at Ole Miss following the court-ordered registration of black student James Meredith.

The shocking violence at Ole Miss was very much on the minds of many

Wallace campaigning in Montgomery in 1958

Wallace in Gadsden in 1962

Alabamians, who did not want to see a repeat if blacks were registered at one of Alabama's public universities. Others urged the governor to stand firm.

Wallace kept to his campaign vows. On a cold January day in Montgomery, after being sworn in on the spot where Jefferson Davis had taken the oath a century earlier as the first president of the Confederacy, Wallace warned that because of a "godless, ever-growing" federal government, the nation itself could become "a mongrel unit," and vowed: "Segregation now! Segregation tomorrow! Segregation forever."

In the strife-torn years that followed, Wallace's administration and his legislative supporters worked to keep that vow. Meanwhile, through the growing medium of television, the nation and world looked on.

In the Legislature, the Wallace forces passed laws to nullify federal desegregation guidelines and created two anti-desegregation agencies that had power to spy and conduct investigations—the state Sovereignty Commission and the Commission to Preserve the Peace.

In the spring of 1963, when the Southern Christian Leadership Conference pressed its campaign to integrate Birmingham's public facilities, Wallace criticized civil rights leader Martin Luther King Jr. and the business group that negotiated a settlement. He also filed suit against the use of federal troops to quell the unrest.

Wallace gave his famous 'Segregation now...Segregation forever,' speech at his first inauguration.

Wallace Family first Inaugural Dance.

New York, June 3, 1963—Three views of Wallace as he appeared with Lawrence Spivak on "Meet the Press" in New York. Wallace told the nation he would do all in his power to keep negroes out of the University of Alabama despite justice department efforts to barr him from interferring.

Wallace's behavior, in turn, drew sharp criticism from some Birmingham leaders and law enforcement officials. So did some of the actions taken in Birmingham by state troopers under the rough-and-tumble command of state Public Safety Director Al Lingo.

Again and again Wallace was at the center stage of resistance and his actions brought letters full of praise or condemnation.

"Please! Please! I pray you, don't give in. You are the last hope of the South and of our great nation," a Mississippi couple wrote.

"The time has come to rid the American stage of men like you who will lead us and our great country further down the road to shame and disgrace," wrote a Massachusetts woman.

The Birmingham crisis barely had been settled when Wallace moved to carry out his principal campaign pledge.

On a blistering hot June 11, an unsmiling, ramrod-straight Wallace, flanked by state troopers, blocked the door to Foster Auditorium to Deputy Attorney General Nicholas Katzenbach and black students James Hood and Vivian Malone.

But by this time, the stand was more symbolic than substantive.

Wallace and Attorney General Robert Kennedy had worked out an agreement by which he would make his stand, President

> *In the name of the greatest people that have ever trod this earth, I draw the line in the dust and toss the gauntlet before the feet of tyranny, and I say, segregation now, segregation tomorrow, segregation forever!*
>
> —January 14, 1963 inaugural address

John F. Kennedy would federalize the National Guard and Maj. Gen. Henry Graham, the state adjutant, would ask Wallace to move out of the doorway.

It went according to plan. As the news cameras rolled, Wallace made his stand, then stepped aside to allow the court-ordered admission of the black students.

As the start of the 1963-64 school year neared, tension mounted around the state as Wallace vowed to continue his attempts to thwart school desegregation. Ultimately, he sent troopers to block the entry of black students into public schools in Tuskegee, Birmingham, Huntsville and Mobile, but those schools were desegregated under federal pressure in early September.

Even that was overshadowed by the Sept. 15 Sunday morning bombing that killed four young girls at Birmingham's Sixteenth Street Baptist Church.

Wallace called the act "a tragic event" and posted a $5,000 reward for information leading to the arrest and conviction of the bombers.

But those gestures did little to change his image in the eyes of many.

Time magazine put Wallace on its cover, called Alabama "a dark, brooding state," and said Wallace was in many ways a "first-rate governor," but that he had become "the symbol of the demagogic segregationist" in the South.

King felt Wallace bore his share of the blame for the Sixteenth Street tragedy. In a telegram to the governor, he said, "Your irresponsible and misguided actions created. . . the atmosphere that has induced continued violence and now murder."

In 1964, Wallace made a brief presidential bid, but by 1965, civil rights events back home were pulling him toward even more notoriety.

In Selma, the west-central Black Belt's largest city, demonstrations had been under way for weeks against voter-registration practices that discriminated against blacks.

King and the SCLC thought the response to the Selma demonstrations would give the nation another dramatic example of racism and spur more corrective federal action.

With a big assist from Dallas County

> *There's no integration anywhere in the world that's working.*
>
> —Wallace during a September 1963 interview with *Time* magazine.

Mrs. Wallace announces her candidacy for governor on Feb. 24, 1966.

Sheriff Jim Clark and Al Lingo, Wallace did not disappoint. As demonstrations, arrests and angry confrontations grew in Selma and nearby Marion, he publicly criticized the civil rights activists, saying they were the cause of the trouble.

Like Birmingham, Selma fueled national outrage. State troopers and other lawmen attacked, clubbed and tear-gassed civil rights marchers at the Edmund Pettus Bridge over the Alabama River, halting a planned trek to Montgomery.

Eventually, several thousand demonstrators completed the Selma-to-Montgomery march. Under prodding from President Lyndon Johnson, an aroused U.S. Congress passed the Voting Rights Act a few months later.

In Alabama, the Selma crisis, like the one before it in Birmingham, prompted concern about the state's image and its ability to attract businesses.

In April, 22 major Alabama business groups, including the state Chamber of Commerce, bought full-page ads in national newspapers calling for equal treatment of blacks.

Lurleen's Term

By 1966, having failed in his push for a law to let him serve two consecutive terms, Wallace ran his wife for governor.

Her campaign was a thinly veiled copy of her husband's. She pledged to "Stand

Wallace does the talking, Mrs. Wallace listens at Ensley...One of five appearances by governor on Labor Day holiday, 1966

Gov. and Mrs. George C. Wallace pause to pose for photographers on the Barbour County Courthouse steps after casting their ballots in 1966. Mrs. Wallace went on to be elected the first woman governor since Mrs. Miriam Ferguson went out of office in Texas in 1935.

> *There's a professor out in California that advocated revolution. Said, we ought to burn the town down. Well, I can tell you this: If any professor in Alabama advocates burning the town down, my little wife's going to see to it that he's a fired professor.*
>
> —Wallace, early in the the '68 presidential campaign

Mrs. George C. Wallace as governor of Alabama

Up for Alabama," and one of her campaign ads included footage of her husband's stand in the school-house door. She won in a race which lost a major moderate competitor. De-Graffenried, making a second bid for the governorship, died in a 1966 plane crash while campaigning.

Her husband, who was to be her chief adviser, made plans to mount a presidential bid in 1968. In the waning months of his term, he kept up the fight against the feds, ordering the resegregation of the state's mental hospitals and signing another bill declaring U.S. school desegregation guidelines unconstitutional.

He also assured public school officials he would make state money available to them so they could offset any loss of federal funds because of their refusal to follow desegregation guidelines.

Mrs. Wallace vowed to continue the battle, but the federal courts continued to topple Alabama's school segregation laws.

A little over a year after her inauguration, with more battles still ahead, Mrs. Wallace died of cancer. She was succeeded by Lt. Gov. Albert Brewer, who spoke in a lower, less-defiant tone of voice.

In 1970, bidding again for the governor's chair, Wallace took aim at some familiar targets—federal judges, for example— and added some new ones such as the Nixon administration and busing to achieve school integration.

> *To ask us to educate our children, classroom for classroom, with a race that is two years behind at the sixth grade and three years behind at the 12th grade, is to ask us to deprive our children of the education to which they are entitled.*
>
> —Wallace in a speech at Harvard University in 1963

Wallace and Brewer, before bitter political fight, enjoy moments together with former U.S. Rep. Tom Bevill.

Presidential hopeful Rev. Jesse Jackson with Gov. George C. Wallace before holding a news conference at the Capitol in 1983.

"Every time a scalawaging federal judge buses a student, he does so in violation of the law," Wallace said at a rally in Fairfield.

Because of increased registration under the Voting Rights Act, blacks were voting in the 1970 Democratic primary in unprecedented numbers. When primary results were in and Wallace found himself trailing Brewer by 11,000 votes, he quickly blamed his second-place finish on "bloc voting."

Everyone knew what the code words meant. Wallace forces used racial smear sheets and talk of a "bloc vote" during the month-long Democratic runoff.

"You! You!" a Wallace runoff newspaper ad screeched. "Not since the 1870s have the people of Alabama been dominated by the Bloc vote. (The word "bloc" was enclosed by a square.) Can the Bloc vote elect a Governor in Alabama? Vote Right—Vote Wallace!"

The message worked. Wallace won the runoff, and used part of his 1971 inaugural speech to decry "despotic and centralized government." But the speech ended on a conciliatory note as Wallace said, "Our state government is for all—so let us join together, for Alabama belongs to all of us —black and white, young and old, rich and poor alike."

Nonetheless, Wallace made an anti-busing law a high priority, and at his urging the Legislature passed a measure banning mandatory school busing. A federal court later declared the law unconstitutional, but busing remained a

To argue that the Negro with whom we deal has the capacity of the white man, is to argue that the mud and straw huts of Africa are equal to the cathedrals of France. To ask us to educate our children, classroom for classroom, with a race that is two years behind at the sixth grade and three years behind at the 12th grade, is to ask us to deprive our children of the education to which they are entitled.

—Wallace in a speech at Harvard in 1963

Of course I've changed. We live in a time of change, and time changes everything.

—From a 1988 interview

potent issue that Wallace exploited during his 1972 presidential campaign, before an assassination attempt cut the campaign short.

After that, the racial issue seemed to recede into the background, not having much potence during Wallace's easy re-election in 1974 or during his last presidential bid in 1976.

In that term, which was his third, Wallace appointed Birmingham publisher Jesse Lewis as his first black cabinet member. He even pardoned Clarence Norris, the last surviving "Scottsboro boy," after the state Board of Pardons and Paroles found Norris innocent of raping two white women in the notorious 1931 case.

Compared to the "Stand Up for Alabama" tactics of the 1960s, Wallace's appointments and placatory moves didn't command comparable national attention.

By then, the spotlight had moved on. But in his give-'em-hell heyday, Wallace used that national attention as a prime reason to put Alabama's message on prime time—as a presidential candidate.

Little Judge Takes on Big Government

Wallace Pursues the White House

He had a boxer's mug and combative nature, wore shiny, dark suits, scowled more than smiled, and spoke with a twang and twist of language that left no doubts about his rural South roots.

He'd stop in the middle of a speech to spit in his handkerchief.

At a time in the 1960s when many Americans still trusted and believed in the rightness of the federal government, he sneered at its pronouncements and court rulings. He ran a state where many blacks lived in fear, and took a certain pleasure in promoting Alabama's image as a place where a crease on the head from a cop's billy club

Placards sprout above heads of throng which crowded Montgomery's coliseum like political convention...Three hours of music, oratory added to atmosphere of George Wallace political, fund-raising rally.

was the best way to quell some of the social unrest.

Presidential material? You bet.

Far from dropping him in the dustbin of history, Wallace's stand in the schoolhouse door and his throw-down-the-gauntlet rhetoric—all against a recurring background of disorder and disarray in his home state—made him ready for even bigger stages by 1964.

In that year, he made his first presidential bid. It was brief, limited to just three primaries. But the strong reception told Wallace he was onto something. Much to the dismay of the national Republican and Democratic parties, he launched major bids in 1968, 1972 and 1976.

> *I can never lose touch with the people. I am one of them. I will stay one of them.*
>
> —January 1963,
> shortly before his inauguration

The pressure for change and the sometimes violent resistance to it that characterized parts of the early Wallace era in Alabama had counterparts around the nation. To people who faced these changes and didn't like what they saw, Wallace talked like the man who could plug the dike. He capitalized on their worry and anger but, in so doing, became a focus for others whose fears and hatreds needed a target.

By the time Wallace's presidential aspirations were finished, he was ailing and wheelchair-bound.

But much of his agenda—support for law and order and national defense, opposition to higher taxes and such socially explosive issues as court-ordered school busing—in short, an opposition to big government—succeeded in becoming part of the national political debate.

And while that kind of agenda didn't win the White House for Wallace, it won it twice for Ronald Reagan.

"Reagan ran on everything I ran on," Wallace said years later. ". . .He even used some of the phrases I used."

In each presidential bid, but especially in the first three, Wallace found a home among many voters—particularly white Southerners and white blue-collar workers who felt threatened by and strongly opposed the changes afoot in American society.

Wallace begins his 1972 Presidential bid in Florida...in Tallahassee to declare his candidacy.

The '64 campaign

In his 1964 bid, Wallace used as a springboard his outspoken opposition to the 1964 Civil Rights Act, which he said would destroy the country's free-enterprise system. He won 25 percent of the Democratic presidential primary vote in Wisconsin, 30 percent in Indiana and 43 percent in Maryland.

The campaign began in Wisconsin a scant few weeks before the actual voting. Some polls, which he later discounted, gave him little chance.

"He didn't even know where Wisconsin was on the map," said Pete Mathews, the Wallace-backed chairman of the state Senate Finance and Taxation Committee who campaigned with the governor.

Mathews recalled a speaking engagement in south Milwaukee before a large audience of white ethnics, many of them Serbians. Wallace thundered about federal meddling in all areas of life and its intrusions on states rights. He never mentioned race, but he didn't have to, Mathews said.

"The blacks had just begun to move in on (the Serbs') turf," Mathews said, "and if you think the people on the bridge at Selma (in 1965) were upset, they were children compared with the Serbs. The Serbs would be just crazy. The Beatles didn't get a reception like he did."

Almost like an epidemic, an unsettling array of problems was about to break out across the nation in 1964. Among other things, the year saw deepening American involvement in the war in Vietnam and the first of several summers in which riots

Gov. Wallace took time out from state business to bring this bouquet of flowers to Mrs. Wallace, who was recuperating from cancer surgery in a Montgomery hospital. Doctors gave Mrs. Wallace a clean bill of health, saying she may be able to resume normal activities in six to eight weeks. This report was of political, as well as medical, significance, since it was during this period that Mrs. Wallace was hinting she may run for governor to succeed her husband.

The image of Alabama is that it is a part of the country that stands up for what it believes in, that it doesn't let the left-wing vociferous liberals run over them and that we don't believe that everything sent down from Washington comes down from heaven.

—At a 1964 rally at Midfield during his brief presidential primary campaign.

wracked some of the nation's urban ghettos.

To some, Wallace became synonymous with the word "backlash"—white resentment and resistance toward black assertiveness and pressure for equality.

"He demonstrated pragmatically and for the first time the fear that white working class Americans have of Negroes," wrote political historian and journalist Theodore H. White.

Wallace's success drew attention from national politicians. Barry Goldwater, the Arizona senator who would be the Republican presidential candidate in 1964, said, "This is the first time in my life that a man has appeared . . . who might put enough votes together to form a third party."

That third-party presidential bid was four years away.

A Serious Challenge

Wallace said that before his wife, Lurleen, died in the spring of 1968, she urged him to keep taking the Alabama fight throughout the nation. To that end, Wallace activists fanned out in a massive effort to get Wallace's name on the ballot in all 50 states and raise money.

With its assassinations, riots and the quagmire of Vietnam, 1968 was a wrenching and tragedy-filled test of the American political system. In the midst of it all, with a tumultuous presidential campaign, was Wallace.

Many of his rallies mirrored the violent fissures within the country. Melees would break out between his supporters and protesters. Sometimes anti-Wallace crowds chanted "Sieg Heil." From behind a bullet-proof lecturn, Wallace would reply, "Go ahead, you free-speech folks, we're gonna quiet you down after November."

Compared to Republican presidential candidate Richard Nixon and the Democrats' Hubert Humphrey, Wallace—the candidate of the American Independent Party—was easily the most charismatic presidential contender in 1968's general election. His supporters were a sometimes bizarre mix. Veteran actor Chill Wills, the movie voice of Francis the Talking Mule, campaigned with him. Another

. . Well, when I get to be president, I'm gonna call in a bunch of bureaucrats and take away their briefcases and throw them in the Potomac River.

—From a 1968 campaign speech in Indiana

Third party presidential candidate George Wallace chats with his running mate, former Air Force Gen. Curtis E. Lemay in Atlanta, Ga., as they go over campaign plans.

backer was white supremacist J.B. Stoner, who called Wallace the "Last Chance for the White Vote."

Chopping the air to make his points, sneering at hecklers as though he'd love the chance to tussle with them, Wallace vowed to shake "the eye teeth" of liberals in both parties.

Wallace talked law and order and urged a tough stand in Vietnam. And, to a greater degree than Nixon and Humphrey, he attacked the federal government, calling it meddlesome and out-of-touch, with its rule-making bureaucrats and heavy-handed federal judges.

Yet in line with Wallace's oft-stated concern for the little man, the Wallace party platform called for boosts in Medicaid and Social Security benefits, along with federal job training for the poor and public employment.

Wallace rallies often featured songs by the Taylor sisters, Mona and Lisa, wearing candy-striped dresses with the governor's picture on the front. Years later, Lisa would become Wallace's third wife.

Wallace's presidential running mate was his old commanding general from World War II, retired Air Force Chief of Staff Curtis E. LeMay.

At the start, the pair didn't seem to be quite in step. No sooner had the announcement been made at a Pittsburgh press conference than LeMay said he would use nuclear weapons, if necessary, to win in Vietnam. "I don't believe the world will end" if that happened, he said. Sensing trouble, Wallace tried to intervene, but LeMay persisted, saying that even though he might not use nuclear bombs, he wouldn't want to tell an enemy that.

Theodore White felt that in choosing the gruff, outspoken LeMay, "the essence of the military establishment," Wallace misread his constituency, which was heavy with enlisted men who never lost their dislike for military brass.

> *I can take anything you anarchists can dish out. You remember that.*
>
> —Wallace at a '68 campaign appearance, responding to protestors who threw an object

In September, however, Wallace was causing the nation's political establishment to worry that he might win enough states to

Gov. Wallace prepares to address state Legislature with smiling Mrs. Cornelia Wallace by his side.

Wallace sports a new look—softer, dryer hair and more stylish dress—as he addresses a joint session of the Legislature. Pierre Pelham, Lt. Gov. Jere Beasley and Sage Lyon are seated behind him.

throw the election into the U.S. House of Representatives.

His voter support had jumped from 9 percent in the spring to 21 percent by mid-September.

But his choice of LeMay, relentless media coverage that showed disorder stalking him wherever he went, a major effort by the AFL-CIO to raise questions about the labor climate in Alabama, and blunt criticism by Humphrey undermined him.

In the end, Wallace carried only Alabama and four other Southern states—Arkansas, Georgia, Louisiana and Mississippi.

Still, the Wallace-LeMay ticket received nearly 9.9 million votes, or about 13.5 percent of the total cast, and 4.1 million of those came from Northern or Western states.

Political observers said Wallace had established himself as a force to be reckoned with.

"What George Wallace demonstrated was that of all those alienated with the set of American government, perhaps the largest were the white workingmen of America," White wrote in his account of the '68 campaign. "And in so demonstrating, George Wallace uncovered a reality that will be of concern for years."

'Sending a Message' in '72

Any doubts that Wallace might return for the 1972 presidential campaign vanished after he recaptured his primary political base—the governor's chair—in 1970.

In January 1971, shortly after starting his

Some time before Gov. Wallace was shot, a man identified as Arthur H. Bremer was questioned by Kalamazoo police on a "suspicious person" report four hours before Wallace addressed a rally there. Police also identified him as the man joining in the applause, but at the time were satisfied with his statement that he had arrived early to be sure of a good seat in 1972.

second gubernatorial term, Wallace opened the national headquarters for a third presidential campaign. At his side was one of Big Jim Folsom's nieces, Cornelia Snively, a former professional water skier whom Wallace had married Jan. 4.

His big issue in 1972—one that had helped him win back the governor's office in 1970—was federal judges busing schoolchildren "to kingdom come."

His slogan was "Send Them a Message," and he walloped 10 other Democratic candidates in Florida's presidential primary, not only opposing busing but supporting heavier taxes on the rich and crackdowns on crime.

With Cornelia's influence, Wallace seemed more polished, better groomed. His wardrobe, mostly beetle-black suits and skinny, dark ties before, brightened to powder blue or grey coats and wide, patterned ties. His slick pompadour became softer and wavy, and he grew sideburns.

Though many rallies were as raucous as those of 1968, politicians and the press regarded him as a serious candidate.

Democratic candidates such as Sens. Hubert Humphrey, Henry Jackson and Edmund Muskie acknowledged voter concerns over the issues Wallace had raised. Nixon strategists worried about Wallace's appeal to northern voters.

At the end of May, he was second only to eventual nominee George McGovern in

"Pressing the flesh" with voters was in important part of Wallace's presidential campaigning style. It helped Wallace build his image of being of the people, but made security personnel nervous.

the number of delegates he had won. But by then, the violence that had swirled around Wallace for so long finally claimed him as a victim, and his chances for the presidency, however slim they might have been, were over.

Appointment in Laurel

Nearly a decade earlier, several days after John Kennedy was gunned down in Dallas on Nov. 22, 1963, a staunch Wallace admirer from Tallassee wrote a letter to the governor urging him to "be careful, for there is more than one Oswald in the country."

The letter was filed away with stacks of other correspondence, its warning long forgotten by the chaotic spring of 1972, when its eerie prediction convulsed into reality in a Maryland shopping center parking lot.

Wallace's schedulers hadn't originally intended for him to go to Laurel, a bedroom community on the northeastern rim of the Washington, D.C., beltway. Maryland was shaping up as a sure win for the governor, and the plan was to wrap things up with a Saturday rally in Frederick, three days before the May 16 primary. Stops in Laurel and nearby Wheaton on May 15 were added to the schedule only two days before they were to take place—"frosting on the cake," as Wallace put it.

His speeches against busing, against

allowing Supreme Court decisions to dictate federal laws, and against anyone who opposed the Vietnam War had drawn mixed reactions from Northern crowds. In Frederick, there was loud applause, but also hecklers and protesters who pelted Wallace with apple cores, stones, and a brick that struck a glancing blow to his chest. There had been anonymous bomb threats days earlier at his stops in Hagerstown and Baltimore.

As a presidential candidate, he was protected by Secret Service agents who traveled with him and who, along with his own state security detail, attempted to limit his random handshaking forays into sometimes hostile crowds. Earlier in the year it had been suggested that the governor wear a bullet-proof vest, but Wallace rejected the idea because the garment's confining bulk would limit his movement.

His Secret Service agents were concerned about the last-minute additions of Laurel and Wheaton to Wallace's agenda, worried they wouldn't have time to inspect the sites and take security precautions. But they grudgingly went along with the plan.

Wallace flew home to Montgomery on Saturday after the Frederick appearance,

Secret Service agents scan the crowd as Wallace doffs his coat shake hands and meet his supporters. The photo was taken only moments before the governor was shot.

A 21-year-old Arthur Bremer yelled, 'Hey, George, let me shake hands with you,' and started firing.

intending to return to Maryland for the final two rallies before the election. He was tired but upbeat. His son, George Jr., who had been singing and playing his guitar to open some of the rallies, had had a startling dream a week earlier in which he'd seen his father mortally wounded by a gunshot to the throat. Young George, then 20, was upset enough by the dream not to play that night, but his father didn't put much stock in premonitions.

Wallace almost canceled the trip, though, when a mix-up delayed his flight crew by about an hour at the Montgomery airport Monday morning. Told that the crowds would still be waiting for him, he resigned himself to going.

Angry protesters were waiting in Wheaton, launching a barrage of tomatoes, eggs and nail-embedded soap cakes that Trooper E.C. Dothard, chief of Wallace's security detail, batted away with a campaign sign.

Near the front of the crowd stood a

Wallace's wife, Cornelia, throws herself over the fallen politician in the Laurel, Md., parking lot.

young man with close-cropped blond hair, wrap-around sunglasses, a dark jacket festooned with Wallace campaign buttons and a strangely vacant smile. Witnesses and photos would place him at a string of earlier Wallace appearances in Michigan, and at President Richard Nixon's visit to Ottawa, Canada, in mid-April.

After a quick hamburger lunch, Wallace was driven to nearby Laurel, where a friendly crowd of about 2,000—a sharp contrast to the surly audience in Wheaton—had gathered in a shopping center parking lot to hear him. He spoke for about 50 minutes, urging them to "shake the eye teeth of the Democratic Party" by voting for him. Afterward, Wallace headed for the motorcade, but clapping and shouting admirers beckoned him and he shucked his coat and reversed his steps, murmuring to his concerned security men, "I believe I'll shake some hands. I'll be all right. I'll take the responsibility."

With Dothard on his left, Secret Service Agent Jim Nobles on his right, and Agent

Nick Zarvos with his back to the governor, Wallace began working his way along a line of spectators in the muggy afternoon heat, reaching out with both hands to shake those reaching for him. From his right, a voice shouted what sounded like, "Hey George, let me shake hands with you." He turned and started to stretch out his hand, but instead of an empty palm reaching to meet him, a stubby black .38-caliber revolver jutted through the crush of bodies and five shots cracked in rapid succession.

Wallace spun to his left as bullets slammed into his right arm, shoulder and stomach. His knees buckled and he crumpled to his back on the warm asphalt, a crimson stain blossoming on his light-blue shirt, just above the waist. Zarvos also fell gasping with a bullet in his throat. Another round hit Dothard in the stomach, and another grazed campaign worker Dora Thompson's leg.

Nearby, security officers wrestled the gunman, Arthur Bremer, to the ground. The 21-year-old Milwaukee man, a former busboy and janitor, had plotted for months in rambling diary notes to kill Nixon and then himself in a bid for notoriety and revenge on society. He apparently switched

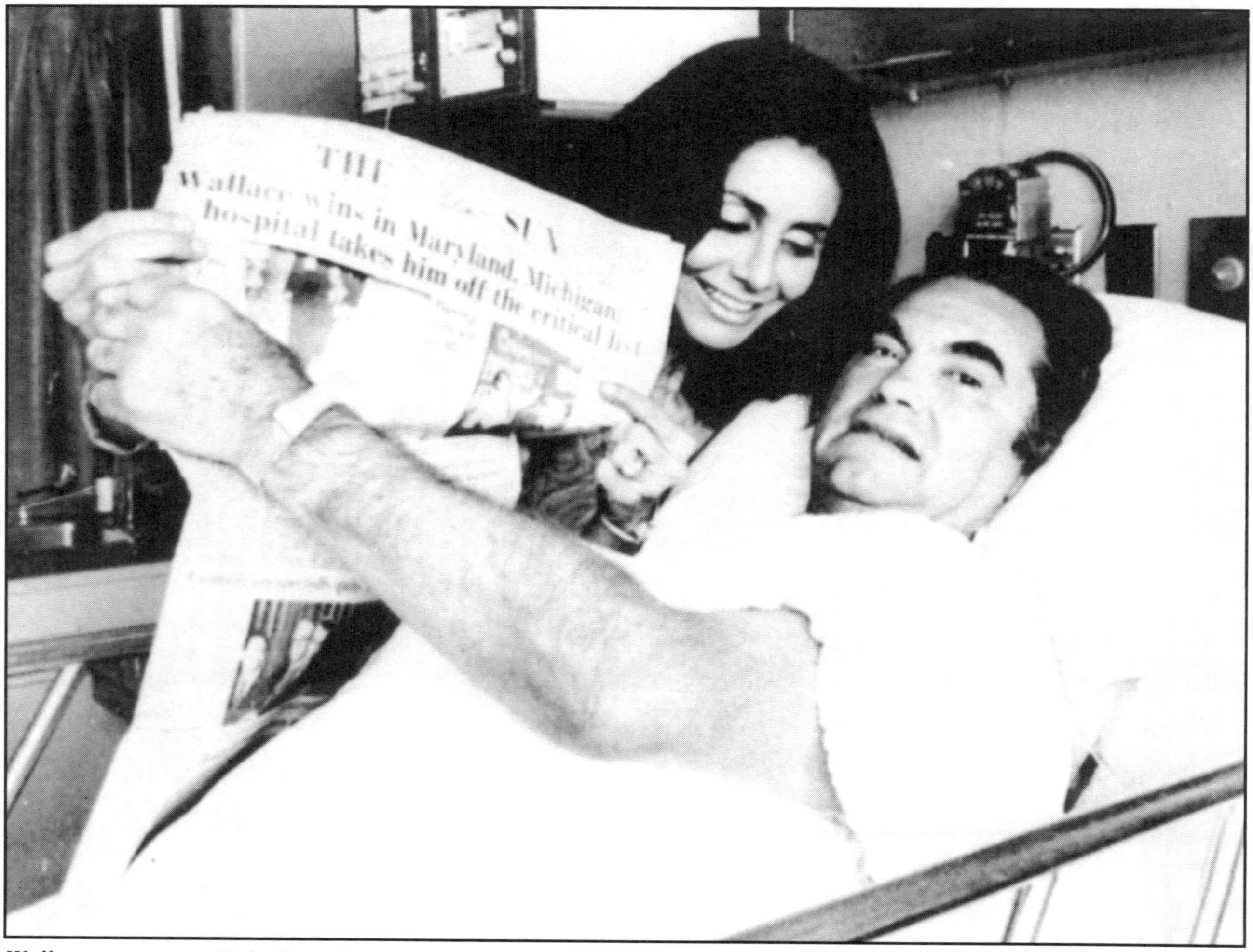

Wallace recovers at Holy Cross hospital in Silver Spring, Md., while he and Cornelia read about his primary victories.

A gaunt, still recovering Wallace presents his party platform views to delegates in Miami Beach from his wheelchair, only weeks after being shot.

to Wallace as a target when he realized the difficulty in getting close to Nixon.

Wallace lay face up, his arms outstretched, conscious but feeling nothing, fully expecting to die. He tried to move his legs but couldn't. Cornelia appeared above him, shielding him with her body and whispering, "You're going to be all right honey. I'm going to take you home and out of all this."

The ambulance ride was a long 25 minutes to Holy Cross Hospital in Silver Spring. The pain escalated from a trickle to a flood, but Wallace remained awake, at one point rising up a bit to ask where he'd been shot, and at another glancing over and gesturing an "OK" sign at Dothard, lying next to him. Still, Wallace believed he was dying. He caught a glimpse of vivid green trees and thought, "Those are the last trees I'll ever see in my life."

"What a sorry way for it all to end," he whispered to himself. Images of the Kennedy brothers and Martin Luther King flashed through his mind, as did his family and Lurleen's dying words: "We will all meet in heaven."

At the hospital he was rushed into

Early 1976 polls showed Wallace second only to Sen. Edward Kennedy as likely contender.

surgery to stop the bleeding in his abdomen, repair the section of intestine torn by one of the slugs, and mop up the toxic contents that had spilled into his belly.

Doctors decided for the time being to leave the bullet lodged next to his spinal cord. It was already clear that he was paralyzed from the waist down, probably

Democratic Presidential candidates prepare for TV taping. (Seated: Wallace; standing, from left, Henry Jackson, Frank Church, Morris Udall, Jimmy Carter.

permanently.

The day after the attempted assassination, Wallace won the Maryland and Michigan primaries.

He stayed at Holy Cross seven weeks, fighting infections caused by the intestinal wound. But he had vowed to attend the Democratic National Convention in Miami and won permission to go. He landed in Montgomery for a brief speech and to comply with the state law preventing lengthy out-of-state absences, then flew on to Miami.

> *All they see is the spokes on my wheelchair, the television catches every one. You've got a man standing up saying, 'Big government is eating you up.' And you got a man in a wheelchair, all humped over, saying the same thing. It's hard to beat.*
>
> —Wallace discussing his chief disadvantage against Jimmy Carter during the 1976 Democratic presidential primary campaign

After Wallace dropped out of the race in 1976, Jimmy Carter paid a visit to the governor while on the way to the Democratic nomination and, ultimately, the White House.

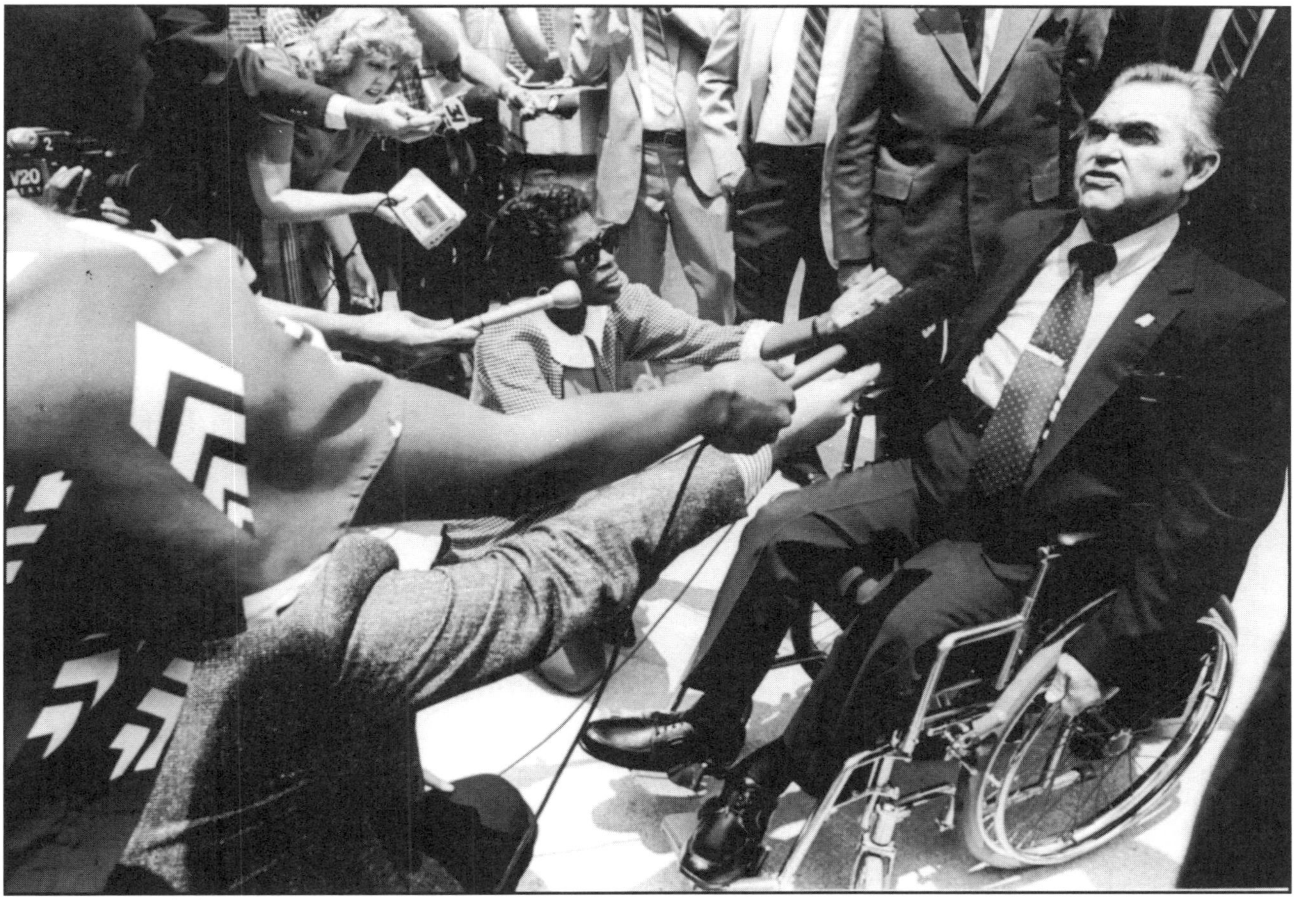

Wallace found the wheelchair to be a serious political liability. It not only hindered his mobility, but also created an image that was opposite of Wallace before he was shot.

Wallace was wheeled into a tiny holding room beneath the speaker's podium in the packed convention center. He waited there in stifling heat for nearly an hour, weak, in pain, at times fighting to stay conscious.

"It was hotter than the dungeons of hell," said friend and cabinet member Taylor Hardin, who was with him. "He held on. I don't know how. Him in that wheelchair, gaunt and tired but waiting to go on. He gave a pretty good speech, but there was no thrust to it."

Not quite six months later, in assessing his resounding general election defeat by Richard Nixon, George McGovern said his own campaign had been mortally wounded by the shooting of Wallace.

Those bullets, McGovern reasoned, ended any chance of a third party bid by Wallace and allowed his supporters to be effectively courted by Nixon, whose administration had proposed a busing moratorium earlier in the year.

Wallace himself thought that, if not for the assassination attempt, "I would have been on the ticket either as the presidential or vice presidential candidate and would have been elected in either spot."

Beaten by the wheelchair

By May 1973, Wallace seemed to be close to his former self. By June, when he discussed the 1974 governor's race, he said, "I'll be healthy enough to beat anyone who runs against me."

There were some encouraging signs about his presidential prospects in 1976. One likely Democratic contender, U.S. Sen. Henry Jackson of Washington, called him "eminently qualified" to be president or vice president, and some polls showed him second only to Massachusetts Sen. Edward Kennedy among likely Democratic contenders.

But this Wallace presidential bid would fail, partly because he had a well-organized and determined opponent in a fellow Southerner and former governor, Georgia's Jimmy Carter.

In contrast to Wallace, Carter came across as a moderate, fresh face. He also was healthy.

"Wallace himself was his own worst advertisement," political reporter Jules Witcover wrote. "Everywhere he went, he had to be lifted in and out of his wheelchair and he had either to speak from it or to be laboriously, and very visibly, taken from it and propped up at the special lecturn. He had underestimated this political handicap."

"The wheelchair beat us," acknowledged Lloyd Jemison, a former state trooper who was one of Wallace's longtime security aides.

Wallace also found Carter a hard candidate to attack.

At one point, he resorted to calling him "a warmed-over McGovern" and criticizing him for hanging a portrait of Martin Luther King in the Georgia Capitol.

It did little good. In such states as Florida, Michigan and North Carolina, where he had won easy primary victories in 1972, Wallace lost to the Georgian in 1976.

By June 8, the surprising Carter had more than 1,000 delegates, and Wallace threw his support to him.

Now, with two years left in his gubernatorial term, it was time to consider the limited political options left to him.

As it turned out, the battered warrior would, with help from a surprising source, have one last hurrah.

Playing games with the press

It was a line George Wallace always could rely on to rile up a crowd.

"There they are out there—the *Newsweek* and the *Time* and the *Los Angeles Times*," he would say, pointing at the reporters who followed him during his presidential and gubernatorial campaigns of the late '60s and early '70s. "You know what they're going to write about you all, don't you?"

Wallace's supporters would jeer and cheer, delighted at how their candidate stood up to the big-city press. The reporters, for their part, usually just smiled. They knew Wallace, for all his hyperbole, would be only too happy to sit down and talk with them afterward.

In public, Wallace portrayed himself as at battle with the press—particularly the national media. In private, however, he was only too aware of how he needed newspapers and magazines and television news broadcasts—particularly those of national scope—to bring his message to potential voters.

"He loved us," said Claude Sitton, who wrote about the South for the *New York Times* in the late 1950s and early 1960s. "He loved publicity. He ate it up."

The publicity was often negative, as reporters who covered Wallace tended to be appalled by his political views. But Wallace was adept at making his point, even in the most adverse of circumstances.

"That was the secret of his success,"

After Wallace got out of the hospital, he tried standing at the podium with help from several straps...within a few months he gave that up.

said Ray Jenkins, a former editor at the *Montgomery Advertiser* and *Alabama Journal*. "The press set out to make him look like some rustic bumpkin, some sort of fire-eating segregationist that attended lynchings. And Wallace was just too smart for them."

Even when reporters did portray him as rustic bumpkin, Wallace was getting his message across to sympathetic readers.

"The media, probably myself included at that point, would write these things like 'the pointy-headed intellectuals who don't know how to park their bicycles,' " said William Greider, who reported on Wallace's 1970 run for governor for the *Washington Post*. "They were great lines, and you would write them in the spirit of 'Listen to what this buffoon is saying now,' utterly unaware that of course Wallace was communicating exactly what he meant."

On television, where Wallace's message didn't have to go through the filter of a reporter's typewriter, he was even more effective.

"He played sort of the little country boy when he was on TV," said longtime NBC News correspondent Richard Valeriani. "So the northern reporters would go after him like a pack of dogs and he'd come off sympathetic."

Wallace first became a nationally prominent figure in fact, on the strength of a June 1963 appearance on NBC's *Meet*

Candidates begin the long wait in Wisconsin...From left, Hubert Humphrey, Henry Jackson and Wallace watch a TV monitor in Milwaukee

the Press in which he defended his stand against the integration of the University of Alabama.

"Everybody assumed that he'd end up doing just like (Mississippi Gov.) Ross Barnett did the year before, blustering away and getting tongue-tied," said Emory University history professor Dan Carter, who recently completed a biography of Wallace. "What Wallace did was he seized the initiative immediately, ignored the questions for the most part, as (other politicians) eventually learned to do—that is pay no attention to what the question is and answer the way you want to answer and say what you want to say."

What Wallace was trying to communicate was a very simple message—it's us against them, and Wallace is on our side.

"Here he's taking on the liberal establishment of the Democratic Party," recalled Jim Wooten, who covered Wallace for the *Huntsville Times* in the 1960s and 1970s. "The next time it's the media establishment he's taking on. And the next time it's the story about how he always took on the banks and the utilities. It was always combat. The context was always combat, and the message was always, 'I'm a fighter.' "

So even when reporters were critical of Wallace, he knew his fighting words were still getting through to potential voters, and thus rarely got angry about the coverage he received.

Wallace did get steaming mad when he felt a reporter had underestimated the size of a crowd that showed up to hear him speak.

"That made him furious," said *Los Angeles Times* reporter Jack Nelson, who often found himself at the receiving end of Wallace's ire for other reasons as well.

Nelson, a Talladega native, quoted Wallace in the vernacular, leaving in slang words and improper grammar—and replacing letters Wallace didn't pronounce with apostrophes.

Like any politician, Wallace didn't like it when reporters held him to account for what he considered off-the-record banter. One day during the 1972 presidential

Presidential candidate Wallace holds a well-worn sandal presented to him in Atlanta by newsmen who had been travelling with him. One of Wallace's favorite retorts to hecklers was, "Come on up here and I'll autograph your sandal." This sandal bears the signatures of all the newsmen aboard the campaign plane in 1968.

Wallace greeted by spectators as he enters the state Capitol in 1978.

Wallace at an 1984 press conference

campaign, for example, Wooten wrote on the front page of the *New York Times* that during a conversation on his campaign plane, Wallace had referred to black U.S. Sen. Edward Brooke of Massachusetts as a "nigger."

"He went absolutely bananas . . . and held a press conference to deny that he'd called Ed Brooke a nigger," Wooten said. That night, however, Wooten says Wallace's wife, Cornelia, told him, "Well, I heard him say it. If nobody else did, I heard him say it."

For the most part, though, Wallace "thoroughly enjoyed jousting with the media," Jenkins said. "Because he knew that he was smarter than the average reporter."

Wallace loved to let his supporters know this. A story he told and retold on the campaign trail was of a televised roundtable discussion in Portland, Ore., in 1964, during which an exasperated journalist said, "Governor Wallace, you must think you're the smartest man in the world."

"I'm not the smartest man in the world," Wallace responded, according to the account remembered by longtime campaign aide Charles Snider. "I'm not the smartest man in the United States. I'm not the smartest man in Oregon. I'm not the smartest man in Portland. I'll tell you one thing, though, I'm

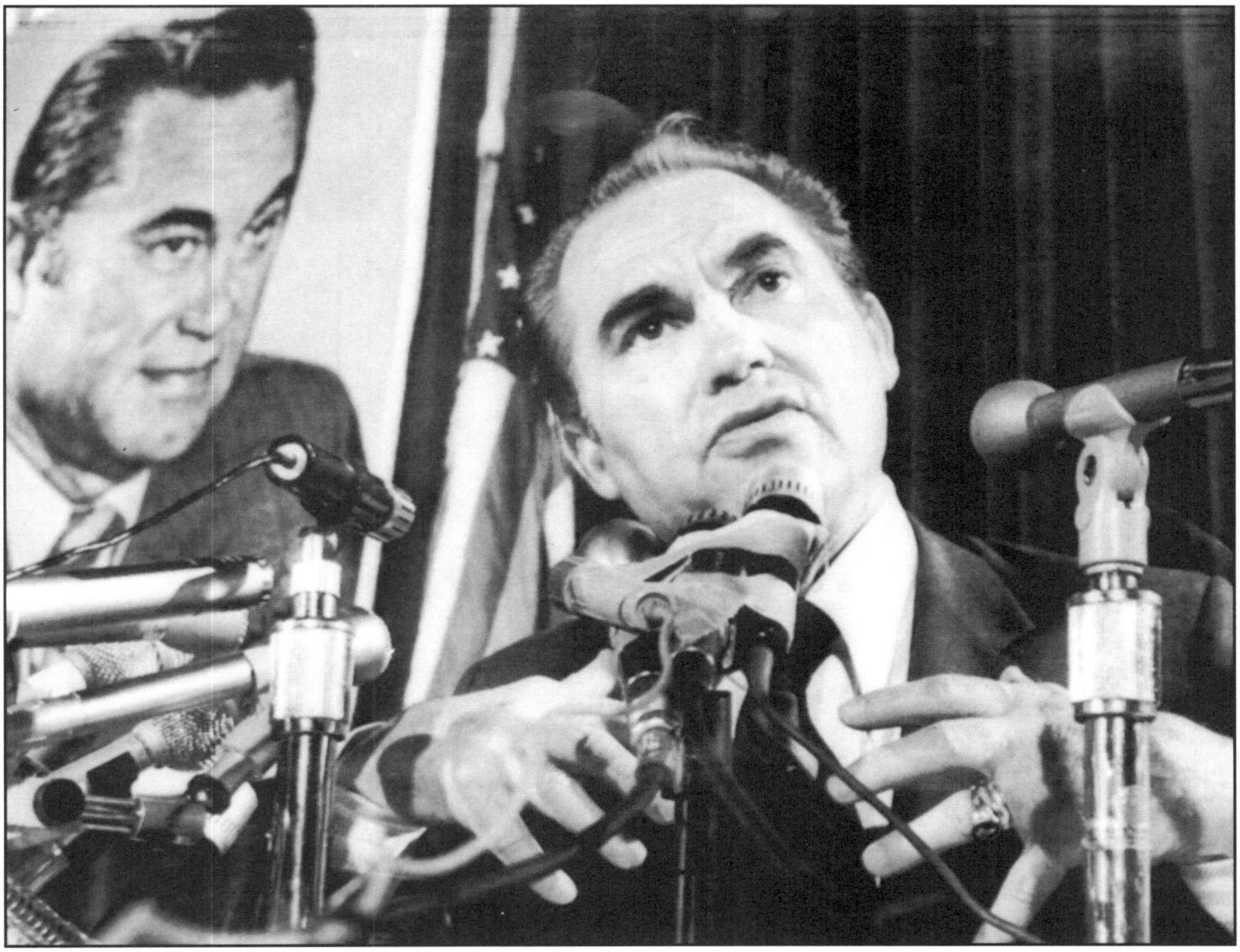

Gov. George Wallace meets the press for a question and answer period after a victory in the Democratic primary.

the smartest man sitting at this table."

But Wallace was too calculating to see reporters only as the potential butt of his jokes. He knew what the media could do for him, and reporters say he was always keenly aware of when deadlines were and how many viewers or readers a broadcast or publication reached.

This awareness led him to favor out-of-towners at the expense of the Alabama media, most local reporters felt.

"He catered to the national and electronic media because that would get him publicity outside of the state," said longtime *Birmingham News* political reporter Al Fox. "He didn't have to worry about getting support in Alabama."

For the reporters, Wallace's attraction was that, with his controversial statements and often bizaare actions, he was always a good story. "I made you, didn't I?" Wallace said to Wooten in the late 1970s.

"He was absolutely right," agreed Wooten, who went on to work as chief

Microphones overflowed the podium as the press followed virtually every move of the governor and presidential candidate.

congressional correspondent for ABC News. "I did make my reputation as a reporter with Wallace and civil rights. There's more to it than that, but certainly I don't think I would have had as interesting career as I've had had it not been for George Wallace. Because he was a terrific story."

The Final Years

On a cold mid-January morning in 1979, a subdued George Wallace sat before a second-story window in a downtown Montgomery office building, watching bands and floats snake through the streets below. He puffed his cigar in silence. The rest of the office's occupants left him with his thoughts.

As outgoing governor, he could have followed the tradition of watching his successor's inaugural parade from the outdoor reviewing stand. But this time, private citizen Wallace shunned the limelight.

It felt like the end of an era. Since the 1976 presidential campaign, Wallace had largely faded from the national political landscape. At home in Alabama, Wallace was prohibited by law from seeking a third

Wallace spent his last election night at home. This photograph was shot as Wallace watched returns showing him trailing Lt. Gov. George McMillan in the Democratic runoff. Two television stations projected Wallace as the loser at about the time this photo was taken. As it turned out, of course, the projections were wrong, and Wallace won.

consecutive gubernatorial term. Wallace had rejected a bid to fill the U.S. Senate seat of retiring John Sparkman, saying that because of his paralysis, "I wouldn't have wanted to live alone in Washington."

If he had gone to Washington, Cornelia Wallace would not have accompanied him.

The two were divorced on Jan. 4, 1978, their seventh anniversary. The split followed four months of charges and countercharges.

So for the first time since 1962, Wallace was not running for governor or president every two years, and faced political retirement alone.

Forest Hood "Fob" James, millionaire businessman and former Auburn football star, won the Democratic nomination and easily coasted to a general

January 1975, former Gov. James Folsom, Mrs. Cornelia Wallace and George Wallace in happier times. Three years later George and Cornelia had divorced.

election victory.

For Wallace, watching James' inaugural procession from afar was a preview of what was to come, a foretaste of the isolation and lack of purpose of life without politics.

He took a job as director of rehabilitation services for the University of Alabama at Birmingham, a $68,000-a-year post in which he spent hours on the phone seeking private donations for various UAB research and assistance programs for the handicapped.

But his political retirement lasted less than a year. Restless, perhaps disappointed with James' rocky first months in office, Wallace dropped hints about seeking a fourth term as early as June 1979. In a college lecture he claimed no political ambitions, but added, "I would never say never."

In an interview a month later, he said, "I miss being governor because I'm paraplegic. I'm busy now, but when I was governor there was something that needed doing 24 hours a day. And someone in my condition needs to be busy. It makes the time pass faster."

In truth, he felt forgotten. "The phone quit ringing," said George Wallace Jr., who lived with him then. "It was tough."

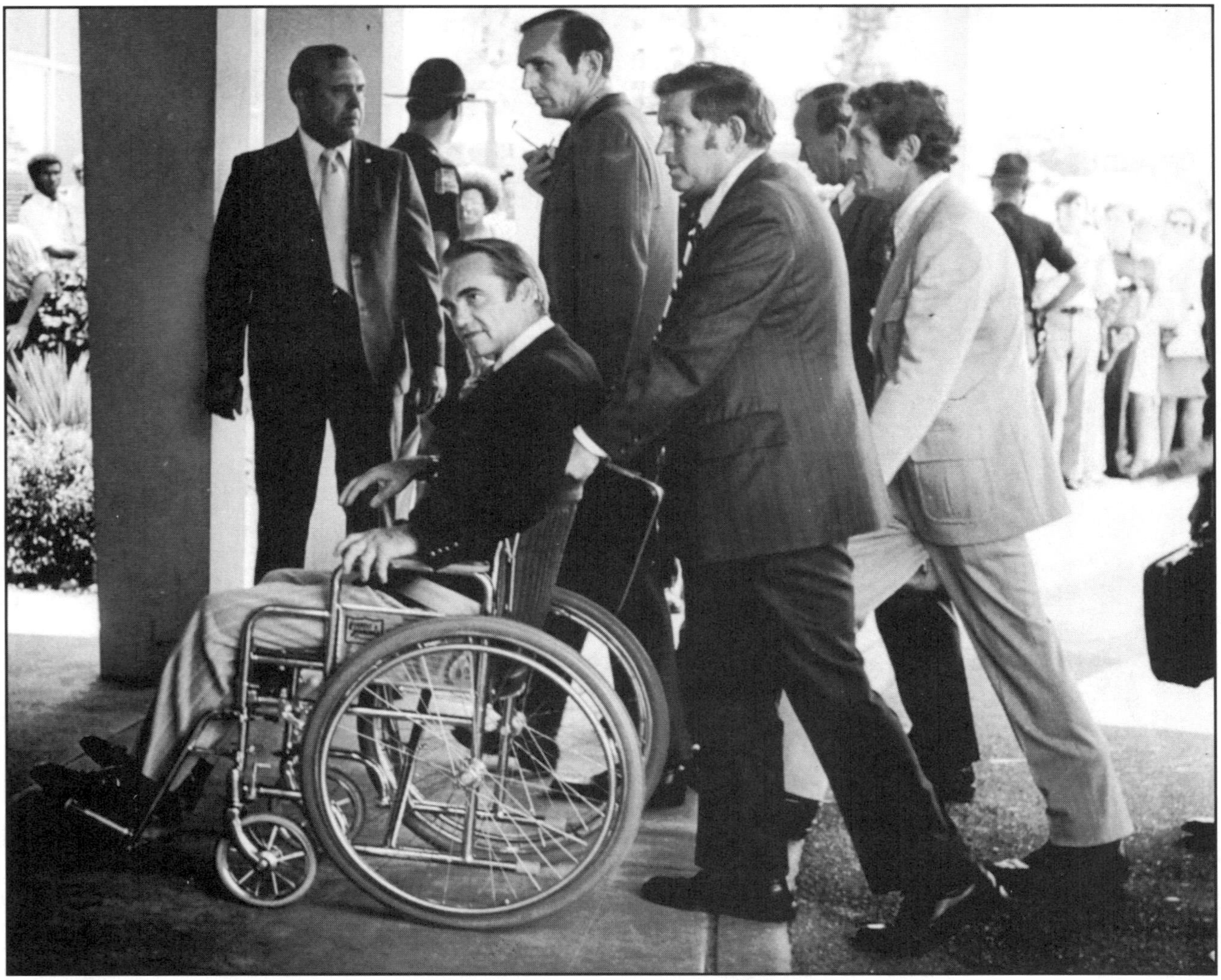

Wallace at Spain Rehabilitation

"He convinced me (running for governor again) was a matter of life and death, that he was laying up in the bed without anything to do and that he'd just die," said his longtime friend and cabinet member Taylor Hardin. "Maybe he was right."

Wallace also said he was rejuvenated by his marriage to his former campaign singer, Lisa Taylor, in July 1981. The wedding between Wallace, 61, and the blonde 32-year-old daughter of a millionaire Jasper coal mine operator surprised even close friends of the governor.

So once more the slumbering Wallace campaign machine was roused, primed and jump-started—the bumper stickers and yard signs were printed, the letters seeking contributions were written, the volunteers tapped, the agenda planned. But still there was some unfinished business to take care of.

Blacks had increased their political power and sophistication through the 1970s and would play a significant—perhaps

Lisa Taylor Wallace and George Wallace during 1982 race.

George Wallace at home before the 1982 election returns talks to reporters about tackling state problems.

deciding—role in the 1982 Democratic gubernatorial nomination. One '82 contender in particular, Lt. Gov. George McMillan, an energetic young progressive, could be counted on to attract black votes. And journalists were certain to bring up Wallace's segregationist past.

All that added up to a pressing need for Wallace to make an open appeal to black voters. In the past decade, he already had softened the edges of his earlier racial comments, starting with his "Alabama belongs to all of us" inaugural remarks in 1971.

But by 1979, Wallace backed away more. On segregation, he now said: "I was raised that way and believed that way. We thought it was in the best interests of all concerned. But I was wrong. Now, anybody that wants it back that way ought to have his head examined."

On the schoolhouse door stand: "I was younger and a little brash. I should have known that some things I was doing would be taken as racist, although I never meant them to be."

At the Alabama Black Mayors Conference in November 1981, Wallace got a standing ovation and a certificate of recognition for his assistance to blacks. Tuskegee Mayor Johnny Ford said Wallace "stands for the common man, both black and white," and that "we have had differences in the past, but the past is the past."

"George Wallace made some mistakes, sure," said Robert Strickland, a 1982 Wallace voter who had been part of the Selma-to-Montgomery civil rights march 17 years earlier. "But he's like Saul, who was struck down and then got up to do good."

Not all blacks were so accepting of the kinder, gentler Wallace.

"I believe George Wallace has changed," Martin Luther King's widow, Coretta, told Selma blacks before the 1982 election. "But if Martin were here today, he would be discouraged that blacks were supporting the man who in the '60s had tried to block their legitimate rights."

But Wallace's conversion didn't prove to be the dominant issue of the '82 campaign. Voters had Alabama's ravaged, recession-strangled economy on their minds. Unemployment was soaring past 14 percent, Birmingham steel mills were struggling, and rural jobs were vanishing.

On the stump, Wallace hit old themes, blaming lenient judges for crime increases, but he conjured up images of better economic times during his past terms and said his international reputation would help lure new business. In sometimes rambling speeches, he'd talk about accomplishments and reminisce about visiting foreign dignitaries. What other candidate could roll up to the British Prime Minister's office and chat with Maggie Thatcher, he'd ask the crowds. Asked what connection those memories had to what he could deliver now, Wallace snapped, "You can tell the future by the past."

His campaign paid for an advertising supplement stuffed in Alabama newspapers that touted the economic progress of

Wallace's three previous administrations. Skeptical reporters found glowing Wallace figures on income and new job rates—which a campaign researcher said had come from newspaper stories—were much higher than those compiled by the state and federal government.

Though the economy seemed to be the spotlight issue, questions about Wallace's health and his fitness for office shadowed him too. At speeches, he retorted that he was only paralyzed in the legs, but that a lot of other politicians were "paralyzed in the head," a remark that brought guffaws from the faithful.

Aware of whispers about his mental status, Wallace quipped after one abrupt transition between topics in a speech, "I'm not incoherent. I'm just trying to say things fast."

Still, there were awkward times. In several speeches he promised to repeal the "good time" early prison release law that had been repealed two years earlier.

Governor and Mrs. Lisa Wallace enter the high school auditorium for the inaugural concert in '83.

"Maybe it was the old warrior's campaign—that people owed him that," Hardin said. The last administration was sort of, 'Let's get it over with.' "

With many rural blacks added to his usual coalition of rural and blue-collar whites, Wallace finished first in the September 1982 Democratic primary. He won 25 percent of the state's black vote but couldn't gain an overall majority, and headed into a runoff against George McMillan. Three weeks later, with about 33 percent of his vote coming from blacks, he squeaked by McMillan with a 19,000-vote margin, the toughest challenge since he won his first term. Wallace carried most of the Black Belt counties, with urban blacks going with McMillan.

The runoff victory pitted Wallace against Emory Folmar, Montgomery's tough-talking, pistol-packing Republican mayor.

Many blacks who didn't relish the thought of voting for Wallace saw little choice with Folmar running. The state's oldest black political group, the Alabama Democratic Conference, reluctantly endorsed Wallace as part of a straight Democratic ticket in the general election.

Wallace swamped Folmar by a 3-to-1 margin, winning by about 200,000 votes, claiming 90 percent of the black turnout.

The Wallace inauguration on Jan. 17, 1983, was a subdued, low-key affair—no traditional parade or ball. The governor was sobered by task force reports on Alabama's crippled economy. He told people to stay home and save their money.

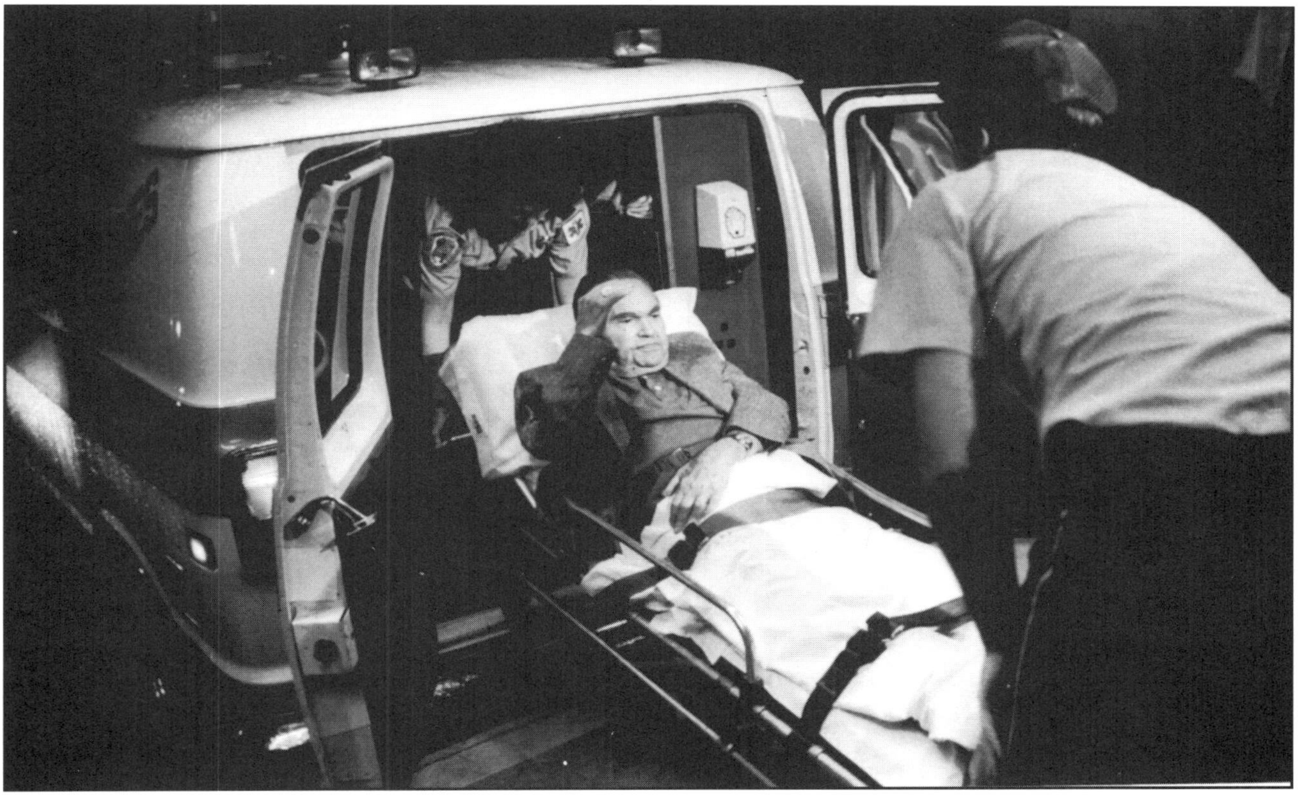

A frail and ailing Wallace at the VA Hospital in 1989.

The reports painted a grim picture—thousands of homeless and jobless people, assistance agencies overwhelmed, schools limping along on a bare minimum of state funding because of the antiquated tax structure, businesses reluctant to locate in the state because of its under-educated workforce and anti-business laws.

The recommendations were the same as those made in earlier Wallace terms, and the same as ones that would be proposed but not substantially acted on throughout the remainder of the 1980s—reform of the tax system, improvement of education funding and quality, revamping and de-politicizing the state's industry-recruiting efforts.

A month after the inauguration, Wallace entered the hospital for the first of what became a string of stays totaling more than 70 days in his final term. The illnesses ranged from intestinal and urinary tract infections, common in paraplegics, to treatment of chronic pain and depression.

During the campaign, when Wallace was regularly on display, there had been a drizzle of questions—mostly from reporters—about his health. His post-election ailments caused him to be cloistered behind hospital doors and turned the drizzle into a torrent of speculation.

The incident that damaged Wallace's image as a healthy governor for the rest of his term happened in March 1983.

Complaining of increased pain from the old bullet wounds, Wallace arrived at Birmingham's University Hospital seeking relief.

The spinal nerves damaged by Bremer's bullets had always caused the governor some discomfort; he frequently could be seen gripping his side or his thigh.

He adopted a short working day, often showing up after noon. His staff explained he spent mornings working at home. During the first months of this term, Wallace was spending even less time in the office, but until now he had publicly downplayed the pain and said he took no medication stronger than aspirin. What some observers saw as occasional mental confusion at Wallace's infrequent public appearances, his aides and doctors attributed to his growing deafness.

But a medication checklist—left on the dashboard of Wallace's limousine on that March day when he arrived at the hospital—indicated that the governor's problems were more serious. The list showed large prescribed doses of two anti-depressant drugs and smaller doses of a narcotic painkiller. Wallace's doctor confirmed that the governor had been depressed for several months—a fairly common condition among paralyzed people—because of governing and personal problems.

Rumors raced through the State House that Wallace was talking of resigning. His staff denied that, but George Wallace Jr. later said his father had been overwhelmed by the state's problems.

"It just got him so down that we, as his children, got with him and told him that he needed to take it one day at a time," the younger Wallace said, "and he settled down to that."

Wallace faced tough economic problems in '84.

Wallace eventually returned to his office, though he spent less and less time there, preferring instead to work the telephone at his home.

By mid-1984 it was apparent that Alabama's economic recovery was happening much slower than anyone had expected; in April of that year, the state still had the nation's third-worst unemployment rate. Alabama's strapped financial status forced Wallace to backpeddle on a key campaign promise not to raise "consumer" taxes.

Wallace asked the Legislature to hike taxes by about $300 million from a combination of income, property, gasoline and license tag fee increases. He insisted that the proposals weren't "consumer" taxes, because they targeted specific groups of people, while "a consumer tax is where everybody pays." The major components of the tax package died in the Legislature.

Wallace wasn't done with surprises that year. In October, after having shunned the Democratic National Convention in favor of an industry-hunting tour of Europe, the state's highest-ranking Democrat shocked fellow party leaders by saying he didn't plan to support presidential nominee Walter Mondale.

The governor later said he had been jesting and without mentioning Mondale by name, made a lukewarm pledge to support "the Democratic ticket." If Wallace was teasing with the non-revelation of his presidential choice, he was downright exasperating when it came to disclosing his own political future. Throughout 1985, he'd drop broad hints that he'd decided to run one day, then the next day he'd say he wanted to put his name on the ballot only if he could be assured of winning.

By fall, the obstacles in his political path were growing. In July, though fearful of further surgery, he'd consented to an unconventional operation to ease his worsening leg and abdominal pain. Denver surgeons deadened his spinal nerves with zaps from electrically charged needles, and prescribed exercises to strengthen his back muscles. The pain lessened, but never completely disappeared. Also, a flurry of late summer and early autumn polls showed a majority of Alabamians felt Wallace was past his prime and were opposed to another Wallace term.

Still, the old master strung out the suspense.

Finally, months past the time that other candidates had gotten campaigns under way, Wallace scheduled an announcement for the afternoon of April 2. He prepared two speeches, one saying he was entering the race, the other confirming retirement. Even George Jr., running for state treasurer, didn't know his father's plans.

Supporters wearing "We Luv Our Guv" pins and reporters packed into the old House chamber, where Wallace had begun his political career as a legislator nearly four decades earlier, and waited for him to be wheeled up to the microphone stand. The crowd of about 300 applauded as he arrived, then the room fell silent except for the whirring of cameras.

Wallace throws a kiss to supporters Thursday after announcing that he would not seek a record fifth term as governor.

His opening remarks were so neutrally worded that Wallace was more than a minute into his speech before it was clear that he had decided not to run again. His voice, a soft, halting shadow of the cannonade of segregationist defiance at his inauguration 23 years ago, began to break.

"Those five bullets gave me a thorn in the flesh as they did the Apostle Paul, and I have prayed that they should be removed, but they were not. I realize, in my own mind, that although I am doing very good at the present time, as I grow older, the effects of my problem may become more noticeable and I may not be able to give you the fullest measure that you deserve from a governor throughout another term.

"In light of this, and after much prayerful consideration, I feel that I must say that I have climbed my last political mountain." Murmured "No's" and muffled sobs broke the crowd's silence. Wallace pressed on, speaking in almost a monotone, trying for perhaps the first time in his speaking career to purge the emotion from his words.

"But there are still some personal hills that I must climb," he continued. "But for now, I must pass the rope and the pick to another climber and say, 'Climb on. Climb on to higher heights. Climb on until you reach the very peak. Then look back and wave at me, for I too will still be climbing.' . . . And while I may be tempted to dwell in the past and say, 'Oh, what might have been,' I must realize, as Peter the Great did, that it is time to lay aside that which can never return and think about the future. And now, I conclude by telling you that my heart will always belong to Alabama. I expect to be around, the Lord willing, a few more years.

But as for the governmental and political arena, my fellow Alabamians, I bid you a fond and affectionate farewell."

True to his word, Wallace vanished from the political landscape after leaving the governor's office in January 1987.

He began working on his memoirs and took a public relations and fundraising job at Troy State University's Montgomery campus, but with increasing pain and deteriorating health, spent much of his time bedridden in his suburban Montgomery home. An attendant and state troopers were with him around the clock.

Wallace's hearing worsened so that telephone conversations—for so long his

May 15, 1986—Former four-term Alabama Gov. George C. Wallace as he salutes farewell to supporters after a tearful announcement that his political career was over.

Wallace during the 1987 inauguration ceremonies of new governor Guy Hunt.

stethoscope to measure the pulse of Alabama's body politic—were virtually impossible. Doctors considered surgically implanting a kind of crude bionic ear, but settled on a modified hearing aid that Wallace said helped somewhat.

In 1990 Wallace seemed to bounce back. He began to take more short trips, traveling in the back of a specially equipped black van to Clayton or Clio for surprise weekend visits or just riding around the countryside. He showed up at the dedication of a new Barbour County prison in the spring and warmly greeted old friends and neighbors.

In early November he even re-emerged—briefly—in the political arena, recording a radio endorsement for Democratic gubernatorial nominee Paul Hubbert. His slurred, weak voice shocked people who had not heard him in recent years.

While Hubbert's bid against Republican incumbent Guy Hunt fell short, George Jr. faced no GOP opposition in winning a second term as state treasurer. On Jan. 14, he was sworn in by his father, just as he had been in 1987.

"I think my son has made a good treasurer during the last four years . . .," Wallace said in part. "He might make a good something else one of these days, also."

Wallace surfaced sporadically after that, making public comments in 1991 about the Persian Gulf War and the 50th anniversary of Pearl Harbor, and saying he couldn't support the presidential candidacy of David Duke, whom some had compared to Wallace.

"I wouldn't be for a former Kluxer," Wallace said. "And I wouldn't be for anybody who ever thought Hitler was a good man, because I almost lost my life in World War II several times . . ."

Though Wallace seemed to enjoy these brief moments back in the spotlight, he didn't seem terribly eager to have them.

"I'm just tired of being on programs," he said during a December 1991 interview. "It's nothing new to me. I was on Meet the Press 13 times, Issues and Answers 13 times and Face the Nation 13 times, so I've had all that I want and I don't want to be in the public light."

In that public light, his suffering and frailty were on display.

Personal Glimpses

By Tom Gordon and Betsy Butgereit
News staff writers

A short while before his death, George Wallace asked old college roommate Glen Curlee to protect his place for posterity.

"Curlee, don't tell everything you know about me," Curlee, who died a few years ago, recalls Wallace saying.

With Wallace's long life, a lot of people know a lot, and some of them were willing to share their memories and impressions.

—Of his fondness for hamburgers, milk and ketchup.

—A campus fight that broke his hand.

—His telephone-itis and the ways he used it to politick and impress.

—His love of politicking, and his fear of not drawing a crowd.

What follows are some anecdotes about well-known and lesser-known sides of George Wallace, from his pre-political years until his final days in Montgomery.

Loving that ketchup

"George Wallace could live on a hamburger and a bottle of milk and a bottle of ketchup," former Sen. Earl Goodwin said recently. "A lot of people said George Wallace put ketchup on ice cream, but he wouldn't do that, that I know of."

Well, maybe not ice cream, but how about cherry pie? the Late Sen. Bob Wilson remembers a day that he and his brother, Jim, then a Walker County circuit judge, ate lunch with Wallace in the governor's office.

"He ordered up from the cafeteria down

Wallace, the young Golden Gloves boxer, puts on a strong performance

there," Wilson recalled. "We . . . had a big vegetable plate and he had a hamburger steak. They sent up cherry pie and I hope to die if he didn't put ketchup all over the cherry pie."

> *No one can be rich, as long as there are those among us who are hungry.*
>
> —Fourth inaugural addresss, Jan. 17, 1983

Boxing with a broken hand

One day while they were undergraduates at the University of Alabama, Curlee and Wallace happened upon a big white youth beating up a smaller black youth. Wallace broke up the fight, but not before he and the bigger youth had exchanged punches. In the process, Wallace broke his hand, Curlee said, but that didn't stop him from fighting in—and winning—a collegiate boxing tournament that came shortly afterward.

A telephone addict

"I think one of the saddest things in his later life was that he couldn't hear on the phone," former state Sen. Jimmy Faulkner said, "because one of his greatest joys in life was picking up the phone late at night and calling friends all over."

"The thing about him, he'll call you at 1 o'clock in the morning just like he'll call you at 8:30 in the morning," Goodwin said. "Time meant nothing to him. It was all politics."

Chriss Doss, former state legislator and Jefferson County commissioner, was at the receiving end of more than a few Wallace calls, and many would come late at night, just as the late night newscast was ending.

In Wallace's final gubernatorial years, Doss said, the calls became less frequent, "and his talking seemed to require so much effort that it was just tiring to listen to him."

In recent years, Wallace's hearing had so deteriorated that when he placed a call, he had to put an aide on the line to write down the listener's response.

While in his heyday he found the telephone a useful tool to stay in touch with allies and kick around ideas and strategies. He would publicly make use of the device as a politically potent symbol.

During his first term, he kept a nonworking telephone on his desk that came in handy when visitors would come seeking his help and he wanted to leave them with the impression that he was on top of the situation.

"A delegation from Podunk or wherever would come in and want a road or something, he'd pick up that telephone and say, 'Give me the highway director!' " former Sen. Pete Mathews said.

For most of his first term, that highway director was Herman Nelson, and Wilson was on hand when Wallace carried on one of those fictitious conversations.

"He'd pick it (the phone) up and say, " 'Herman, George Wallace. Listen, I'm in conference here with Senator Wilson and

> *Because what happens to my soul is going to be more important than what happens to me in history. I . . . don't think much about my own history. I do know, though, that I've done a lot of things that I don't get credit for.*
>
> —George Wallace in 1991

his group, his highway people from Walker County.' He'd say, 'We been working on that Highway 18 up there. Get your crew up there and let's do something on that, okay?'

"Those. . . folks'd go out just happy as larks," Mathews said, "and the telephone wasn't connected."

Former state Sen. Roger Bedford of Russellville remembers a connected telephone that kept ringing and disrupted an industrial development announcement in Wallace's office during the governor's last term.

After interminable minutes of ringing, Bedford said, Wallace picked up the receiver and said, "Hello, IRS. May I help you?"

Whoever was on the other end didn't bother to answer.

"They hang up every time," Wallace said.

Friendly reporters

Wallace wasn't always sure if he could dominate a press conference, particularly as he moved onto the national stage. So when he could, he would plant some aides in the crowd of questioners and that way he could assure himself of some friendly questions.

Bob Wilson remembers one of those occasions came during a 1968 presidential campaign stop in Manchester, N.H. William Loeb, publisher of the *Manchester Union-Leader*, was pro-Wallace, but before a morning news conference the governor nonetheless had campaign aides Ralph Adams, Schuyler Baker, and Wilson himself hang some press cards around their necks.

During the conference, Wallace took

We were married (almost) 25 years and she was one of the prettiest little teenagers you ever saw.

—George Wallace, recalling his first wife Lurleen

Friends and family join Wallace at his 1973 Birthday party in Montgomery.

Alabama is blessed with an abundance of resources known to few others. Her mines and minerals, her rivers, streams and harbors; her forests, factories and farms; her cities and villages; and, most of all, her people...eager, willing, capable, industrious and determined to create a better way of life for themselves, their families and neighbors. This spirit cannot be extinguished or defeated. We will overcome our problems...

We recognize and applaud the monuments to corporate profit that tower in glass and steel above our cities. We recognize and applaud the desires of those of great individual wealth to build among us monuments to high culture and entertainment. We recognize and applaud the great temples of worship and Christian education that religious denominations seek to build and assert upon our landscape to glorify Almighty God.

But for God's sake, let us also hear the sighs of the hungry and the cold among us. Let us do unto the least of these, and God will reward us with His blessings in His way in His time...Any nation that forgets its poor will lose its soul.

—From George Wallace's
Fourth Inaugural Address

questions about his encounter the night before with protestors at Dartmouth University, but then said, " 'Lemme take this reporter's question over here,' " Wilson said, and he'd turn over there (toward) Ralph Adams and Ralph would feed him a loaded question, you know.

"He'd take another one or two and (say), 'Lemme take this one over here' and I'd give him one . . . We did that for a while. After a while, the press caught on that we might have been more favorable to him than the local press was."

Love of campaigning

Earl Goodwin said Wallace often would be afraid of not drawing enough people to his campaign site.

"He always said, 'Don't get a hall too big,' but we always got the biggest hall we could ever get and when we got that hall, we filled it up," Goodwin said. "I never remember us not filling a place up when we was campaigning for president.

"Yet he was afraid of not having a crowd. And he told me one time, 'Crowds are the answer. Crowds are the answer.' And he told me one time, he said, 'Earl, if you're ever campaigning and you're going around on the stump, and you don't get a crowd, pack up and go home, you're through.'

"The only reason George Wallace ever went to football games and all was for the crowds," Goodwin said. One occasion, Goodwin recalled, he and Wallace were at Legion Field, with more than 70,000 in the stands, and Wallace said, " 'You see all those folks up there? There's a lot of those folks (who) know you . . . but every one of them know me.' "

In his own way, Wallace epitomized the truth that for the consummate politician, the campaign never stops.

While on the trail with Wallace, "You'd have to run in and get him a hamburger, and a bottle of milk and some ketchup and bring it out and keep going, for the simple reason that if he went into a restaurant, he never went into a place that he didn't shake hands with everybody in it, the kitchen on down," Goodwin said. "You go into a garage or something, he got right down in the grease pit with the guys. That's the kind of campaigner he was."

One of the dumbest things

The late Glen Curlee believed one of the dumbest things Wallace ever did was to include the line "I draw the line in the dust and toss the gauntlet before the feet of tyranny and I say segregation now, segregation tomorrow, segregation forever," in his 1963 inaugural speech. "This radical fellow up in Birmingham (Asa Carter)" wrote the infamous segregation line, Curlee said, and Curlee begged Wallace to take it out, but he wouldn't.

Wallace and Big Jim Folsom in 1963.

"This will come back to haunt you. Please don't say this," Curlee told Wallace. "But he said it, and it's come back to haunt him through the years."

Wallace refused to delete the line, saying, "That's what the public wants to hear, and it was at that time," Curlee remembered.

Wallace the teetotaler

Curlee remembers his old roommate as a teetotaler. And those teetotaling days started in the late 1940s, Curlee said, after Wallace, then an assistant attorney general, took a sip of something named Green River at a party at Curlee's Montgomery home.

"It made him sick," Curlee recalled, "and he stayed there for three days before he could get up. He said then, 'I'll never touch another drop as long as I live.' As far as I know, he didn't."

A future foretold

During their college days, Curlee remembers a time when he and Wallace were talking about the distant future, and Wallace's humorous description of himself was eerily prophetic.

"I'll be in a wheelchair, and they'll roll me out in the sunshine," Wallace told Curlee, "and I'll be watching the children play, and you'll be out chasing their mommas."

How will history rank George Wallace?

by Dan Carter

What will American historians in the next generation make of the career of George Wallace?

His place in the history of Alabama is not in doubt. His place in our national history is not so clear.

When James G. Blaine, U.S. secretary of state and the Republican presidential candidate of 1884 died in 1893, there was a massive outpouring of grief. Businesses came to a halt across much of America and a state funeral drew thousands of mourners to hear politicians and religious and public leaders vie with each other to describe what one eulogist called "the statesman of our century."

Two years later, America's black community mourned the death of the famous black orator Frederick Douglass with only perfunctory notice from most whites. Today, however, the great black orator who was born a slave sits firmly in the pantheon of America's historic figures. And who remembers Blaine?

The future has a habit of playing tricks on the past. It is ironic that George Wallace began and ended his career as a moderate on race and (by Southern standards) a free spending advocate of government intervention to aid the weak. For his most obvious claim to historical significance lies in his opposition to the civil rights movement of the 1960s.

Nor is it an accident that Wallace burst into national prominence in 1963, the year which was—in many ways—the highwater mark of the civil rights movement.

There is an old Arab proverb which suggests that men are made more powerful by having powerful enemies. Between his

At the Washington reception, the governor is greeted by Sens. Edward Kennedy and Mike Mansfield (right).

January inaugural speech in which he pledged segregation forever, through his June stand in the schoolhouse door, George Wallace's deliberate confrontation with the Kennedy Administration over civil rights transformed him from a marginal, backwater Southern politician into a national figure who commanded the attention (if not always the admiration) of the national media as well as leaders of both political parties.

In the years that passed after his inaugural speech, Gov. Wallace attempted to minimize the importance of race in his rise to power. He was aided in that process by the fact that most Americans and most Alabama voters remembered little about Wallace's inaugural speech beyond his famous line, "Segregation now! Segregation tomorrow! Segregation forever!"

That amnesia has allowed Wallace to insist that his defense of segregation was a symbolic issue, that his struggle was one to preserve states' rights against the overweening power of the federal government.

As he later said on several occasions in attempting to dismiss the significance of his inaugural address, he should have said "states' rights now . . . states' rights tomorrow. . . states' rights forever." He was never against black people; he was simply angry with the federal government and wanted to protect Southern states' rights.

In reality, the defense of segregation was not simply a symbol of larger issues of states' rights; white supremacy lay at the very core of that speech.

In the brief space of less than 20 minutes, Wallace suggested that the Supreme Court was following the communist line, accused the nation's political leadership of having created a "basically ungodly government" which "encourages everything degenerate and base," and claimed that the federal government had betrayed American values by seeking to "amalgamate" the nation into one "mongrel unit" instead of maintaining "each race within its own framework."

At one point in the speech, Wallace even linked the 1962 court-ordered integration of Ole Miss with the 1960 slaughter of white Belgian settlers by Congolese tribesmen.

Never again did Wallace throw to his audiences the red meat of explicit racism, but no one who listened to him in the years that followed would ever doubt the relevance of racial fear and hatred to his appeal as he lambasted "busing" or attacked the "pointy-headed bureaucrats" who were trying to tell employers they had to hire "so many red-headed Baptists and so many Chinese Methodists," or brought an all-white crowd to its feet with a promise that, as president, he would protect their right to control their own "local affairs."

Former Montgomery newsman Ray Jenkins often argued that Wallace's decision to use the race card amounted to a "Faustian bargain" in which he abandoned any long-term national political future in order to achieve success in the racial cauldron of Alabama's 1960s politics.

If so, Wallace never hesitated.

Nor did he hesitate in using race to broaden his appeal outside Alabama. His first great insight, in fact, came with his realization that his message would play outside the South. It was, said one Southern-born newsman, as if Wallace had looked out upon those white Americans north of Alabama in the early 1960s and suddenly been awakened by a blinding vision: "They all hate black people, all of them. They're all afraid, all of them. Great God! That's it! They're all Southern! The whole United States is Southern!"

The late Douglas Kiker exaggerated for the sake of effect, but his point was well taken.

If that were the sum total of George Wallace's contribution to American politics, he would merit little more than a footnote, and an ignominous one at that; to be placed alongside such dusty Southern demagogues as former Mississippi Gov. Ross Barnett and former Arkansas Gov. Orval Faubus.

Wallace understood and capitalized upon the deep fault lines of race in American society, but he also understood that the anger which gripped middle class and working class Americans was something more than racism. As he traveled around the country in the mid- and late-1960s, Wallace sensed a deeper sense of betrayal.

It was not just that blacks were moving out of their "separate station" and challenging the system of segregation. The traditional cultural values which most Americans had accepted seemed under attack: an acceptance of hard work, the centrality of the family, a faith in God, and an unquestioning patriotism (so long as it was associated with conservative values).

Even the post-war economic miracle which had promised higher and higher incomes seemed a sham as working-class Americans had to struggle harder and harder to stay in place.

The 1960s were a whirlwind of change: Lyndon Johnson's Great Society programs, the Supreme Court's decisions outlawing school prayer, expanding the constitutional rights of accused criminals, and ultimately guaranteeing abortion rights for women; the rise in street crime and the decade's race riots; the rise of a political and sexual counterculture which was reflected in the "hippie" movement; and, more politically, in the opposition to the war in Vietnam.

A master at sensing shifts in his listener's mood, Wallace was the first to grasp the breadth and depth of the anger and disillusionment of what later came to be called the "silent majority." From his first foray into the Wisconsin Democratic presidential primary in 1964, when he obtained an astonishing 34 percent of the vote, to his third-party run in 1968 when polls showed him the choice of one out of every five voters, through his last presidential campaign in 1976, Wallace broadened the traditional politics of race to evoke a more general politics of working class conservatism which emphasized protecting cultural and racial values as much as economic interest.

In immediate political terms, Wallace's main contribution seems to have been in mobilizing a constituency centered in the South, but stretching out into the heartland

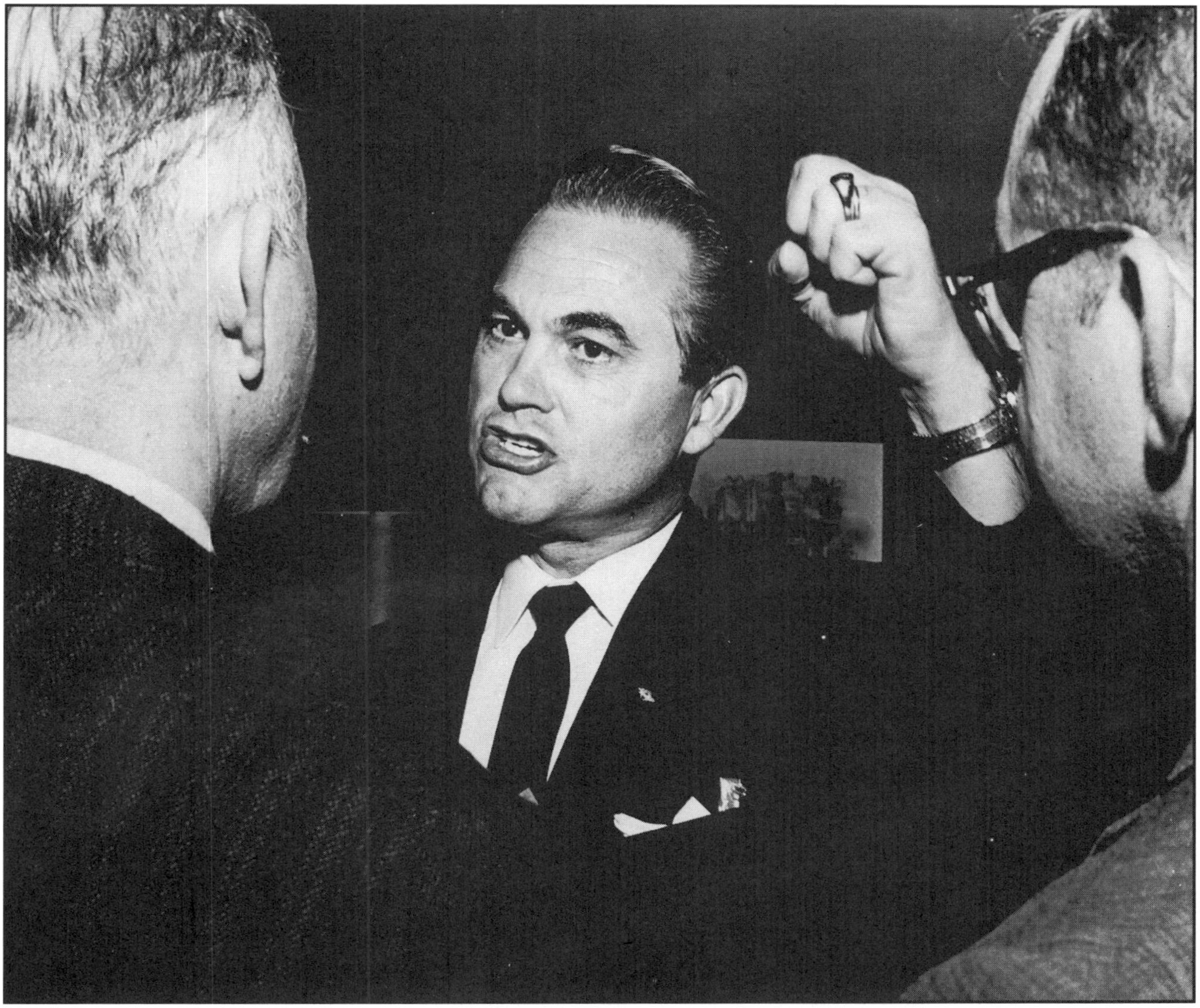

Wallace—always the fighter—makes his point with clenched fist.

of America, which was ripe for the picking in a Republican Party conservatively positioned to take advantage of the cultural and racial conflicts which were destroying the old Roosevelt Democratic coalition.

In that sense, Wallace played an important role as a halfway house for hundreds of thousands of disaffected Democrats (particularly in the South) while on their way out of the political house of their fathers and into the Republican Party.

That is not the historical legacy for which George Wallace yearned. According to his son, George Jr., on the day in 1986 when Wallace announced his decision to retire from public life, he murmured as he rode away from the state Capitol, "I wonder who will look out for the poor people now."

More than a decade before Wallace's death, Clarke Stallworth, a *Birmingham News* editor and writer, asked the four-term governor what he thought the history

Gov. George Wallace in 1963—just beginning the career that would define Alabama policies for a quarter century.

books would say about him. "I would like to be remembered as one who opened up equal opportunity for all people," Wallace replied, as he listed, almost desperately, the various social programs he had undertaken while in office.

The future of those voters whom George Wallace aroused—the forgotten Americans—may be the key to his role in our future history. If that "Wallace" constituency retreats to the politics of scapegoating—to the David Dukes and Jesses Helmses of the 1990s— historians will take little note that Wallace himself turned his back on the politics of race. His role as a demagogic defender of white supremacy will remain our dominant memory.

But, if the working class and middle class voters should reach across the barriers of race at the end of the 20th century and unite in a common effort to remedy the social and economic problems that have plagued America for more than three decades, historians will look with a kinder eye on George Wallace; to judge him for the whole of his career and to take seriously the fretful concern his son says he expressed after deciding to leave politics: "Who will look out for the poor people now?"

The future has a habit of playing tricks on the past.

Achievements

His fiery, defiant rhetoric and the controversial stands he took are the headlines of George Wallace's career.

They tend to overshadow a lot of major legislation that passed during his four gubernatorial terms, as well as the abbreviated one of his late wife, Lurleen.

Some of the Wallace accomplishments stemmed from his years as a legislator—particularly the legislation providing for trade schools and to assist industrial development. Some other significant changes of the Wallace era, particularly in such areas as mental health and prison reform, came from federal court orders, often issued by U.S. District Judge Frank M. Johnson Jr.

Johnson ordered massive reforms in

the state's mental health system, improvements in prison medical care and extensive reforms throughout the state's overcrowded and understaffed prison system.

He also ordered the all-white state Department of Public Safety to hire black state troopers and ordered the Legislature to adopt a redistricting plan that boosted black and Republican representation in its ranks.

Other measures that passed during the Wallace years, such as that which created the state Air Pollution Control Commission, reflected the growing national concern over environmental degradation.

Here's a look at some of the other major legislation—outside the civil rights arena—that passed during Wallace's career:

• **Education**: During Wallace's term as a freshman legislator after World War II, he successfully sponsored the Trade School Act to establish regional vocational and trade schools to equip Alabama veterans and others with the skills to land decent-paying manufacturing jobs.

In his first gubernatorial term, 1963-67, Wallace backed legislation that created the University of South Alabama, funded free textbooks for public school students, and increased the number of junior colleges and trade schools.

During Lurleen's gubernatorial term, 1967-68, legislation established Auburn University at Montgomery.

And in Wallace's last term, 1983-87, the state bought a "supercomputer" to boost higher education and industrial development.

• **Business/economics**: The Wallace Act, passed during Wallace's freshman legislative term, allows municipalities to equip and furnish industrial-development sites and to lease this property to industries. It also allows tax exemptions for industry locating on the site.

In his first gubernatorial term, Wallace supported legislation that raised $100 million for road and bridge construction. During Lurleen Wallace's term, bills passed that authorized large-scale construction and improvements at the Alabama State Docks, and required state banks to pay interest on state deposits.

In the 1970s, voters approved a Wallace-backed constitutional amendment to put a ceiling on property taxes.

And in Wallace's last term, legislation piggy-backing on a concept passed into law earlier with the backing of former Gov. Fob James set up the Heritage Trust Fund to protect and manage money received by the state from offshore oil and gas leases. Also passed was legislation to limit lawsuits that one worker can file against another for on-the-job injuries, legislation backers said would help the state's business climate.

• **Environmental**: During his first gubernatorial term,Wallace established the state Water Improvement Commission to monitor the cleanliness of the state's lakes and rivers.

Legislation during his administration in the 1970s established an Air Pollution Control Commission, and established and improved public parks and recreation facilities.

Wallace and Lurleen after 1963 inauguration.

Wallace and Fob James in 1978.

• **Humanitarian**: During Lurleen Wallace's term, measures allocated more money for mental-health centers and hospitals.

Legislation from Wallace's third and fourth terms set up a Department of Youth Services and an Ethics Commission; exempted from sales taxes all prescription medicines purchased by the elderly; and established a pilot kindergarten program and a health-care insurance plan for the needy.

Also passed during that time: bills expanding teacher retirement and workmen's compensation benefits.

In his final term, Wallace supported bills that established a crime victim's compensation commission and expanded unemployment compensation.

Highlights

August 25, 1919	Born in Clio, in Southeastern Alabama's Barbour County, the first child of George C. Wallace and Mozelle Smith Wallace
1935	Dubbed the "Barbour Bantam," wins back-to-back bantamweight Alabama Golden Gloves championships.
1936-37	Appointed a page in the Alabama Senate
Fall, 1937	Enrolls in University of Alabama. Elected freshman class president in his first successful political campaign.
1942	Graduates from UA law school and enlists in Army Air Corps.
May 21, 1943	Marries Lurleen Burns, a 16-year-old dimestore clerk from Tuscaloosa County.
December 8, 1945	Discharged from Air Corps, returns to Alabama as a $175-a-month assistant attorney general in Montgomery.

May 7, 1946	Wins a seat in state House of Representatives representing Barbour County. Aligns himself with populist Gov. James "Big Jim" Folsom.
1947	Sponsors Trade School Act establishing regional vocational and trade schools.
July, 1948	As delegate to Democratic convention in Philadelphia, opposes Harry Truman's civil rights program, saying it infringes on states' rights. Stays with Democratic Party rather than bolting to separatist Dixiecrat movement.
May 2, 1950	Wins second legislative term at the onset of new administration of conservative, business-oriented Gov. Gordon Persons. Introduces the Wallace Act allowing cities to issue bonds to develop industrial property and providing tax exemptions for industry that locates on land.
1952	Elected circuit judge of Barbour and Bullock counties.
1954	South Alabama coordinator for Folsom's second successful gubernatorial campaign; breaks with Folsom in a dispute over his advisory role and Folsom's cabinet appointments.
August, 1956	As member of platform committee at Democratic convention in Chicago, helps water down Democrats' civil rights plank, adding to his growing statewide reputation as a segregationist and states' rights advocate. Wins another term as circuit judge.
June 3, 1958	Makes first run for governor, but loses Democratic runoff to Attorney General John Patterson in a campaign in which racial segregation is main issue.
November, 1958	As circuit judge, squares off against old college friend and now U.S. District Judge Frank Johnson over possession of contested voting records from Barbour and Bullock counties. Works out an arrangement to turn over the records to federal authorities, but gloats that he defied the federal government and "stood up for Alabama."
June, 1962	Wins Democratic gubernatorial nomination, defeating among others his former mentor, Big Jim Folsom, and state Sen. Ryan deGraffenried, who says Wallace's repeated segregation vows will hasten integration.

January 14, 1963	Inaugurated as Alabama's 48th governor, and vows "Segregation now, segregation tomorrow, segregation forever," charting Alabama's defiant segregationist stand through the next decade.
June 11, 1963	Defies federal court order and fulfills campaign promise by standing in the door of University of Alabama registration building to block enrollment of two black students. President John F. Kennedy federalizes Alabama National Guard and forces Wallace aside.
April-May, 1963	Police clashes with civil rights protesters in Birmingham spark riots and bombings, ending in September bombing of Sixteenth Street Baptist Church, which kills four girls. Wallace says he is growing tired of Martin Luther King and his "pro-Communist" supporters, and opposes intervention of federal troops to quell disturbances.
April-July 1964	Begins Northern speaking tour and enters several Democratic presidential primaries on strength of his schoolhouse door stand and opposition to proposed federal civil rights legislation. Wins 25 percent of the vote in Wisconsin, 30 percent in Indiana, and 43 percent in Maryland.
March 7, 1965	Civil rights activists marching from Selma to Montgomery are attacked, beaten and turned away by Alabama lawmen at Selma's Pettus Bridge. Wallace, who had banned the march, says he deplores the violence but defends the lawmen's actions as necessary for public safety. The incident sparks nationwide sympathy protests and ultimately spurs passage of 1965 federal Voting Rights Act to end discriminatory voting barriers.
October, 1965	Decides to run wife Lurleen for governor after losing state Senate fight to allow a statewide vote on whether a governor can serve a second consecutive term.
November, 1966	Mrs. Wallace wins gubernatorial election. Wallace serves as her top adviser while mounting a second run for the presidency, this time as a third-party candidate. Chooses retired Air Force Gen. Curtis LeMay as his running mate.

May 7, 1968	Gov. Lurleen Wallace dies of cancer after 16 months in office. Succeeded by Lt. Gov. Albert Brewer, a longtime Wallace ally.
February-November, 1968	Wallace mounts spirited presidential campaign, advocating law and order and a drastically less meddlesome federal government. Finished with nearly 14 percent of the vote and carries five Southern states. In Alabama, voters approve constitutional amendment allowing governor to serve two consecutive terms.
June 2, 1970	Wins Democratic gubernatorial nomination after bitter, racially-charged runoff against Brewer.
January 4, 1971	Marries Cornelia Snively, Big Jim Folsom's niece and a former professional water skier. Two weeks later, opens national headquarters for his third presidential campaign. Using slogan, 'Send them a message,' easily wins a crowded Florida presidential primary in which court-ordered school busing is a big issue.
May 15, 1972	Shot by a mentally disturbed gunman, Arthur Bremer, while campaigning in Laurel, Md. Wounds leave him paralyzed below the waist and in a wheelchair for rest of his life. Wins subsequent primaries in Michigan and Maryland.
June 6, 1973	Watergate testimony reveals $400,000 in Nixon campaign funds were used to try to defeat Wallace in 1970, and $10,000 in such funds were used in bid to thwart possible independent presidential bid by Wallace in California in 1972. Wallace's name also surfaces on Nixon Administration "enemies list."
November 5, 1974	Seeks and easily wins third gubernatorial term. Before his inauguration, speaks to congregation of Martin Luther King's old church, Dexter Avenue Baptist, pledging to be governor of all Alabamians. Also pardons last surviving "Scottsboro boy," after parole board finds him innocent of raping two white women in historic 1931 case.
November 1975 - June 1976	Runs for president a fourth and final time, losing in key primaries to the ultimate Democratic nominee, Jimmy Carter.

January 4, 1978	Divorced from wife Cornelia on their seventh anniversary.
January, 1979	Leaves governor's office and goes to work as a fundraiser for University of Alabama at Birmingham.
July 26, 1981	Marries Lisa Taylor of Jasper, whom he met in the late 1960s when she and her sister Mona sang at his campaign rallies.
November 2, 1982	Wins an unprecedented fourth gubernatorial term with help of substantial black vote. In speech to black delegates to Southern Christian Leadership Conference, acknowledges having made "mistakes" in the past in his attitudes and actions on racial matters. During his term, he is hospitalized for extended periods for paralysis-related pain and infections and rarely speaks in public.
November 3, 1990	Announces he will not seek re-election and is retiring from politics. Leaves office and goes into virtual seclusion for a time, rarely leaving his Montgomery home. A week after inaugural ceremonies in which Wallace turns control of the state over to Republican Guy Hunt, Lisa Taylor Wallace files for diverce.
November 3, 1990	Three days before the gubernatorial election, Wallace briefly emerges in a radio ad endorsing Democratic nominee Paul Hubbert, the teacher lobbyist he had had several memorable clashes with over education funding in the 1970s. Hubbert is convinced Wallace can help deliver crucial white votes in the close battle with Republican Gov. Guy Hunt. Hubbert loses the election by about 45,000 votes.
August 25, 1994	Wallace turns 75. Family members reveal plans for a library, research center to honor him and the late Gov. Lurleen Wallace and form a foundation to raise funds to build a center for the Study of Southern Politics.
October 10, 1996	With Wallace attending, the Wallace Foundation presents first Lurleen B. Wallace Award of Courage to Vivian Malone Jones, one of two black students he tried to bar from UA in 1963.

About the Authors

George Wallace: A Portrait of Power was written by *News* staff writer Tom Gordon and former staff writer John Mangels, with contributions from former staff writers Justin Fox and Tom Lindley.

Gordon is a state reporter who covers politics. He joined The News in 1982.

Mangels joined *The News* as a staff writer in 1982. He covered medicine and politics before working as an assistant metro editor. He is now a staff writer for *The Cleveland Plain Dealer*.

Lindley, the former chief of *The News'* Montgomery bureau, is editor and publisher of *The Evening News* in Jeffersonville, Ind. Fox, a former Montgomery reporter and editorial writer, is now a staff writer for *Fortune* magazine.

The concluding essay was written by Dan Carter, a William Rand Kenan Jr. professor at Emory University in Atlanta. Carter is the author of a 1995 biography of Wallace, *The Politics of Rage*.

Most photographs are from the News' files and include the work of Charles Nesbitt, the late Haywood Paravicini, Bernard Troncale, Robert Adams, Ed Jones, Hal Yeager, Steve Barnette, Joe Songer and the late Anthony Falletta. Several photos are by Tommy Giles of Montgomery.